SONGWRITING BREAKTHROUGHS

STRATEGIES AND PROMPTS FOR WRITING YOUR NEXT SONG

SHANE ADAMS

This book is dedicated to Maurgea, Evangelia, and Isadora,
the joy, bliss, and hope of my life.
I love you beyond compare.

BERKLEE PRESS

Editor in Chief: Jonathan Feist

Senior Vice President Pre-College, Online, and Professional Programs/
CEO and Cofounder of Berklee Online: Debbie Cavalier

ISBN 978-0-87639-233-1

1140 Boylston Street
Boston, MA 02215-3693 USA
(617) 747-2146

Visit Berklee Press Online at
www.berkleepress.com

Study music online at
online.berklee.edu

Distributed By

Visit Hal Leonard Online
www.halleonard.com

Berklee Press, a publishing activity of Berklee College of Music, is a not-for-profit educational publisher.
Available proceeds from the sales of our products are contributed to the scholarship funds of the college.

CONTENTS

ACKNOWLEDGMENTS

I would like to thank the following:

- Maura-Lee Albert for her generous support.
- Jonathan Feist, whose wisdom and friendship made this book possible. You've enriched my life.
- My Berklee mentors: Pat Pattison, Jimmy Kachulis, Bobby Stanton, Stephen Webber, and John Aldrich, your positive influence on my life is incalculable.
- My fellow songwriting torch-bearers: Scarlet Keys, Andrea Stolpe, Susan Cattaneo, you've inspired me more than I can express.
- My incomparable Berklee NYC crew: Merrily James, Arun Pandian, Lee Moretti, Rob Mathes, and the rest. I'm amazed at the lot of you.
- Special thanks to Debbie Cavalier for her leadership and vision for Berklee's future.
- My magnificent musician/educator brothers-in-arms Aaron Helvig and Adam Ollendorff at the Country Music Hall of Fame and the Taylor Swift Education Center, I'm so blessed to be sharing the road of enriching the lives of others through better songwriting. Your impact is as immense as your knack.
- Love and respect to Carin Nuernberg, soul sister Susan Lindsay, Matt Iorlano, Camille Colatosti, Sam Charnes, Courtney Kaiser-Sandler, Tom Childs, Ally Lubera, Nick Boyer, Hayley Collins, and the rest of my wonderful Interlochen tribe, I am in awe of your individual brilliance and collective panache.
- Fistbump to my brilliant wingwalking family at Envoy/American Airlines. Tail north on Yankee 3!!
- Love and remembrance to the late Bob Ball who gave a path to my potential.
- Gratitude to Cheryl Syphus for believing in me.
- Warmth and thanks to R.S., your inspiration is a diamond to my madness.
- Thanks most of all to my many students, clients, friends, and family.
- And Sunny. I would never, ever forget Sunny.

FOREWORD

by Jonathan Feist
Editor in Chief of Berklee Press • Songwriter

You are so lucky to be holding this book. Its origins hail from the hallowed halls of Berklee College of Music, where hit-songwriting craft has long been meticulously analyzed and discussed; from the mean streets of Nashville, that no-nonsense mecca of music, where every cab driver is a better songwriter than you are; and of course primarily, from the perspective of a boy who loves a girl, a human spirit who wrestles with angels and demons alike—an extraordinary compassionate person whose heart easily breaks at any story of suffering, who rejoices at the triumph of any fellow creature, and who is compelled to turn all of that into song. Shane Adams can finally teach you that obscure concept in music theory that you never were able to grasp before. And he'll brake for that squirrel crossing the highway, even with you honking your horn behind him. He knows that songwriting is a mystical art, and he treats its pedagogy with the reverence, and perhaps irreverence, that it deserves.

It's been one of the great pleasures of my life and career to have been Shane's coconspirator, for well over twenty years, now. He and I have covered a lot of ground. This is our second book together. We've taken each other's Berklee courses, we've co-taught the same classes, we've presented at the same songwriting workshops. We've written songs together, and even performed together at a coffee house. He's produced me as an artist. I've edited him as an author. I've gone down to Nashville to write songs with him over barbeque; he's come up to Massachusetts to write with me over fried clams.

I've watched him teach many, many times, and I have to say, that's a magical experience that every songwriter should make their life's priority to witness, if you can. Shane comes from the *Dead Poet's Society* "stand on a desk" school of teaching. While grounded in academic discipline and refined in the real-world commercial songwriting industry, his presentation is crystal clear so that you can understand it, and out-of-the-box so that you remember it. I've heard many teachers referred to as Yoda. Some get called that because they are really smart, and perch on your shoulder, and giggle while they beat you up. But Shane is the rare Yoda who lifts your TIE fighter from the swamp with a wave of his hand so that you can go fulfill your destiny. Magical. Practical. Grounded in compassion. Superhuman. Masterful and cool, though what he does is certainly harder than he makes it look. And endlessly entertaining.

I lead a songwriting group, here in Gloucester, MA. Shane visits every now and then to present a songwriting lesson. I'm pretty sure my group would prefer him to me as their leader. For months after his first visit, they were quoting him.

"Shane said this," and "Shane said that"—sometimes even defiantly, as if contradicting the things that I told them. Heck, I actually gave them some of the same advice, months before. But when Shane says it, they think it must be true. Because among Shane's many gifts is that he is likable. An annoying reality, to a natural grump such as myself. It's just that Shane can explain the most esoteric concept of songwriting theory with a clarity and a warmth that simply breaks through, and makes you feel better. When he speaks or performs, the room is enraptured. And when his students go home and write using his unique techniques (which you have at your fingertips right now), their songs take giant steps forward.

Shane's own songs are poignantly heartfelt and meticulously crafted, and he should stop messing around and focus on recording them, for a change, rather than just helping other people write the most beautiful songs of their lives. As is his wont. But that's another story.

In this book, you can bask in the rare pixie dust by that unique educator and human spirit that is Shane Adams. You don't need to read it all at once, cover to cover. Just pick it up, read a lesson, and chew on it for a while. Absorb it into your soul. And write with it. Each page, each idea, can give you a hundred new songs.

Let it do that for you. And if you can, make a pilgrimage to learn from the master in person. There's nobody quite like him.

PREFACE

The topics in this book came about as solutions to problems I encountered while writing my own songs. They materialized after a lot of thought and experimentation, and were refined as I used them with my songwriting students and clients. They are practical in nature, and I found that both seasoned and beginning writers have found benefits in them that they could apply immediately.

For years, I have been sharing these ideas with thousands of songwriters across the globe, and it is exciting to me to have them all in one volume. I hope you will find the techniques, activities, and prompts as useful in your own songwriting.

Remember to always apply the techniques to support the emotional intent of your songwriting, and not the other way around.

Let's go write your next song!

Part I

Lyrics

A song's lyrics are an accumulation of small choices whose sum transcends its parts. The songwriting process often begins with brainstorming story ideas and coming up with an initial set of lyrics that will more or less fit the song's melody and structure. We often find, though, that while these early drafts describe what emotions we are feeling, our actual lyrics don't wind up effecting the listener to the same degree.

When you write songs, you are not just expressing yourself; you are crafting an experience for your listener. While your lyrics don't always have to be soul-wrenching and intimate, you should have control over the intended level of intimacy.

The workshops in this section are designed to help you elevate your lyrics to best serve your intended narrative effect.

CHAPTER 1

Your Favorite Songs

Your songwriting identity eminates from all your favorite songs.

Who are you as a songwriter? You feel compelled to come up with something new, but what is your genre? How can you use your influences but still be different?

You are a wonderfully unique combination of all the songs that you know and love. In the dead center of all those songs is who you are as a writer.

Rather on relying on preconceived notions of what you *think* you should do in a song, let's discover what your favorite songs are *actually* doing musically and lyrically, and then use those elements to craft a uniquely powerful personal style.

ACTIVITY

Create a list of your top twenty favorite songs. For older songwriters, I like to divide this list into two lists: ten favorite/influential songs from when you were a teen (those early songs are incredibly indelible in how our musical tastes were formed) and ten favorite songs as an adult. Choose songs that that have both lyrics *and* music. The songs can by the same artist, or can be different genres entirely. This is all about *your* tastes and strongest influences. We will refer back to your Top 20 list throughout this book.

Next, identify and write down a specific single feature that you love most about each song. Is there a lyric that conveys an emotion that moves you? Maybe the title is showcased in a memorable way, maybe there's a passage of melodic brilliance, or a chord progression that rocks your world. Did something rhyme in a cool way? Is there alliteration that seals the deal?

Put into words one thing that stands out for you and helps you love each song.

YOUR NEXT SONG

You now have a list of twenty things you love about songs. Next, write a song or song section that pivots around something you love. Use the melodic shape, use the chord progression, use the way the title was repeated, etc. Choose one thing you love, and use that as the basis for your own next song.

CHAPTER 2

Lyric Augmenting Using Prosody

Support the emotional lyric intent through prosody.

The word "prosody" means "how words are set" to poetry or music. Prosody was traditionally used to describe a word's natural accent being in alignment with nontextual elements, such as with rhythmic/metrical accent and melodic direction. Songwriters expand this concept to include the alignment of lyrics with any musical construct. For example, when discussing emotional "highs" or "lows," a melody could similarly move in an ascending or descending direction, to subliminally reinforce the concept.

Song prosody mostly occurs subconsciously, but you can choose to apply prosody more deliberately to augment the meaning of your lyrics. Many elements can influence your lyrics' story and emotion. Is the song in a major or minor key, and does that choice best support the lyrics? Is the song fast or slow, is the melody high or low (or both!), does the melody use long or short notes, how often are there words that rhyme? Is there alliteration in the lyric? What's the instrumentation?

There are dozens of possible elements that influence the meaning of your song. The combination of these elements presents the tone and demeanor of how listeners perceive and process your lyric.

Imagine telling someone these words: *It's time to leave*. Do you yell? Are you polite, or sighing with regret? Are you passive-aggressive? Asking a question? Demanding? Maybe someone made a bad joke and you're being sarcastic. It's not just the words "it's time to leave"... it's *how* you say those words.

For a song, the constructional elements (tempo, chord quality, dynamics, key, harmonic rhythm, etc.) are *how* you say the words. If your choices of these elements align with your song's story and emotion, the song's effect becomes increasingly expressive and clear.

This way of aligning song features—prosody—can be a brilliant brainstorming method to connect song lyrics with other constructional elements that support the meaning and message of your lyric. Prosody relationships are little behind-the-scenes Easter eggs that makes a song extra special.

Some examples of prosody in some hit songs:

- "Over the Rainbow" (Yip Harberg, Harold Arlen, from *The Wizard of Oz*). The melodic shape is like a rainbow.
- "Friends in Low Places" (Earl Bud Lee, Dewayne Blackwell; performed by Garth Brooks). The word "low" is set on the lowest melodic note.
- "Another White Dash" (Butterfly Boucher). The white dashes refer to broken lines on a highway, and the way she sings them make them seem like they are flying by as you drive past them.
- "Royals" (Lorde). Whenever she mentions "royals," they are always at the front of the song section, as if they are ahead of everybody else.

ACTIVITY

List several song elements that could create prosody in a song. Here are some ideas, to get you going:

- **Tempo**: Is the song fast or slow?
- **Harmonic Rhythm**: Are chords changing every couple beats or every measure?
- **Chords**: Is there a repeating chord pattern? Do the chords feel tense or relaxed, harsh or pretty?
- **Arrangement**: What instruments are heard?
- **Key**: Major or minor?
- **Lyric Speed:** Are the lyrics sung fast, slow, or maybe both?
- **Melody Notes**: Are they long or short?
- **Melody Shape**: Does the melody only move upwards or downwards? Does it stay on the same note? Does it zig-zag? Does it arch?
- **Feel:** Is the rhythmic feel tight or loose? Is the song bouncy or rigid?

Listen to several songs from your Top 20 list, and consider the story and meaning of the lyrics. What other song construction elements can you identify that help reinforce the lyric's meaning?

YOUR NEXT SONG

Choose one or two types of prosody from the preceding activity. Create a new song or song section using similar lyric/musical element relationships as your starting point.

CHAPTER 3

Song Sections and Stories

The functions of verses, choruses, and bridges.

The different functions of song sections (verses, choruses, bridges) have roots that go back thousands of years. In ancient Greece, a play was divided up into sections called "acts." Acts consisted of actors using action and dialog to present the story of the play. In between each act, a group of singers called the "chorus" performed, and through song, they shared insight regarding the dramatic action of the previous act, which helped the audience follow the performance. This interplay of an act followed by the chorus repeated throughout the play: Act 1, Chorus...Act 2, Chorus...Act 3, Chorus...etc. In this dramatic structure, the responsibility of the act was to move the story forward, and the job of the chorus was to sum up the preceding act. (Note: This is the historical root of the double meaning for the word "chorus": both as a group of singers, and as a section that comments on the main action of a section.)

Songwriters have continued a form of this act/chorus structure to great effect in songs. We move the story forward in one type of section (in songs, called "verses"), and then sum it up in either a chorus or single lyrical line (i.e., a "refrain" line).

In this book, we will refer to three primary types of song sections:

1. **Verse:** A verse moves the story forward.
2. **Chorus:** The chorus sums up the verse and typically includes the title, or hook. (Songwriters typically use the terms "title" and "hook" interchangeably to mean the most memorable line of the chorus, since sometimes the song's actual title isn't used in the chorus).
3. **Bridge:** A bridge has the same role as a verse (to move the story forward) but with different music. It is common for the bridge to replace the third verse before the last chorus. It might bring the story to an unexpected or more emotionally charged place.

Understanding these structures can help your songwriting by planning out the song *before* writing the actual lyrics. Ask yourself, what is the complete story of the song and how can you divide that story up into three or more "acts?" Each act (which will become verses and/or bridge) should contain new information and advance the song/story idea forward without repeating the same sentiments.

Note that these structure types don't only apply to "story songs" with written characters going through situations. A song's "story" can be an emotional journey, or a journey of thoughts and observations. They key here is the each verse has its own separate identity, that is then summed up in the hook or title in a chorus or refrain line.

Here are some verse-chorus songs:

- "You Belong with Me" (Taylor Smith, Liz Rose; performed by Taylor Swift). In the verses, the narrator tells what's going on in the boy's life. In the choruses, she tries to make him realize that he's better off with her.
- "Crazy Train" (John Osbourne, Randy Rhoads, Robert Daisley; performed by Ozzy Osbourne). In the verses, the narrator is coming to grips with a world that is falling apart around him. The choruses repeat the hook/title's metaphor of a crazy train. The bridge is a plea for people to listen to him and change.
- "If I Were a Boy" (Brittany Jean Carlson, Toby Gad; performed by Beyoncé). The verses are about what the narrator would do on a day-to-day basis if she were a boy. The choruses focus on how she would be a better "boy" in a relationship because she knows how it feels to be a girl in a relationship. The bridge articulates her enlightenment that she doesn't want her boyfriend back.

ACTIVITY

Choose a title/hook or central idea for a song, and then describe the song's story in three (or more) sections. These sections don't have to be lyrics yet. They can be just the idea for each "act," which will then become your verses and/or bridge.

YOUR NEXT SONG

Write actual verse lyrics (with or without a bridge) that support each part of the story that you outlined. Use your title as a refrain line or to create a chorus.

CHAPTER 4

The "Mozart Method" for Finding Titles

Use your favorite song lyric to generate inspiring titles and song hooks.

The Mozart Method is a quick and easy brainstorming procedure that produces a huge list of titles. You'll narrow that list down to the best five titles and then choose the one that has the *most* potential and is the *most* inspiring and emotionally connected to what you want to write about.

This title will be turned into a meaningful chorus, which will be the catalyst for the remainder of your song.

The whole process will take only about ten minutes.

THE SETUP

From your Top 20 Songs list, choose one with a lyric that creates the same type of mood/feeling of the song you want to write. Ideally, select a song that is structured as a narrator addressing another character. This lyric will become a letter that is passed between four fictional friends, who will share their opinions about the "letter/lyric" with each other. (Note: Many kinds of text will actually work for his exercise, but choosing a favorite song will help you stay emotionally connected to what you are about to write about.)

THE SCENARIO

In this exercise, you will become four different characters: Mozart, Cleopatra, Gandalf, and Oprah. Use the following scenario prompts to compose their thoughts, advice, interactions, and reactions.

To set the scene, Mozart has written a letter to Cleopatra. The words in Mozart's letter are the lyrics from one of your Top 20 songs. Gandalf (Mozart's best friend) and Oprah (Cleopatra's best friend) will offer advice to Mozart and Cleopatra.

Note: For these four characters, you may choose any names, genders, nationalities, ages, dispositions, attitudes, outlook, quirks, opinions, etc. They can be agreeable or disagreeable. You can even assign them different names if you'd like! These are the ones that I like to use.

Prompt 1: Oprah advises Cleopatra about Mozart's letter.

Cleopatra receives Mozart's letter (the lyrics of one of your Top 20 songs) and immediately shows it to Oprah. Oprah, a true friend, offers brutally honest advice on what Cleopatra should say back to Mozart. Oprah can be antagonistic or agreeable to either Cleopatra or Mozart.

You might consider:

- What does Oprah think of Mozart, the letter writer?
- Is Mozart a positive or negative influence on Cleopatra?
- Is Cleopatra a positive or negative influence on Mozart?
- What does Oprah think Cleopatra should say or do to Mozart?
- How does Oprah think Cleopatra should treat Mozart?

Writing Exercise

You are Oprah. Write your opinion/advice to Cleopatra, for two minutes.... GO!

PRE-WRITING TIPS

You don't need to write actual lyrics in this exercise, or for many pre-writing exercises. There is no need to use rhymes or create a complete story. You certainly can, if doing so flows easily, but it is not a necessary part of the exercise, and you shouldn't let the desire to write actual lyrics slow you down. Instead, for now, you are getting your raw ideas down quickly.

Run-on sentences and incomplete thoughts are okay. There are no right or wrong scenarios.

Trust your first instincts, forge ahead, and see what you come up with. Good luck!

PROMPT 2: Cleopatra replies to Mozart.

Cleopatra contemplates Mozart's original message and considers Oprah's advice. Cleopatra picks up her pen and writes back to Mozart.

You might consider:

- Is Cleopatra angry or happy with Mozart?
- What is Cleopatra's vision of their future and/or feeling about their past?
- What does Cleopatra want, need, or seek from Mozart?
- Does Cleopatra stand up for herself or cave?
- Is Cleopatra antagonistic or agreeable? Combative or forgiving?
- Is Cleopatra shallow or noble, strong, or a pushover?

Writing Exercise

You are Cleopatra. Respond to Mozart for two minutes.... GO!

Prompt 3: Gandalf gives advice to Mozart on his next move.

Mozart receives Cleopatra's message and shares it with Gandalf. Gandalf gives advice regarding Mozart's next move.

You might consider:

- What does Gandalf think Mozart should say and do?
- How does Gandalf think Mozart should react or act towards Cleopatra?
- Does Gandalf agree or disagree with Cleopatra?
- Does Gandalf agree or disagree with how Mozart has been acting towards Cleopatra?
- Does Gandalf have a secret agenda?

Writing Exercise

You are Gandalf. Give your opinion/advice to Mozart for two minutes. . . . GO!

PROMPT 4: Mozart responds.

Mozart replies to Cleopatra.

Consider:

- Does Mozart agree or disagree with what's been said?
- How does Mozart feel?
- Is Mozart deflated or encouraged? Angry or happy? Or in-between?
- What's Mozart's plan, going forward?

Writing Exercise

You are Mozart. Reply to Cleopatra for two minutes. . . . GO!

YOUR NEXT SONG

You now have four (or more!) paragraphs of thoughts and opinions. Search each of the four writing prompts, and underline words, word combinations, and phrases that can be potential song titles. Next, put a star next to any of the underlined potential titles that are particularly inspiring. Now choose the best five title ideas from those you have starred, and list them on a fresh page.

Which of these last five titles have the most potential? Which of these last five titles is the most inspiring to you? Which of these five titles makes you say: Yeah, I want to write *that one*!

Congratulations, *that* title will be your next song!

So, write a new song chorus based on that title. You can repeat it several times or combine it with "swing lines."

If you like, add verses and develop your chorus into a complete song, possibly drawing additional lines or ideas from your Mozart Method writing examples.

WHAT I LIKE ABOUT THE MOZART METHOD

- It's quick! The entire exercise only takes about 10 minutes to complete. (The "actual" writing is cumulatively only 8 minutes).
- It's productive! All five of the titles at the end are potential songs. (Think about it. Combining the Mozart Method with your list of Top 20 songs will generate a minimum of *one-hundred* potential and inspiring titles...more if you include *all* the underlined, potential titles).
- It has side benefits! The phrases and sentences that aren't the chosen title(s) are potential lyrics.

CHAPTER 5

Manipulating Title/Hook Placement

Maximize the impact of your title/hook on your song's narrative.

Lyrics are meant to be heard, not read. Understanding how our brains process what we hear can help us maximize the impact of our lyrics.

Listening is managed by a psychological phenomenon called the *primacy/recency effect* (also called the *serial-position effect*), which emphasizes and creates an importance for things you hear first (primacy) and last (recency), with the "first thing" having a slightly stronger impact.

Every line of a song section, such as a chorus, thus has a first and last impression for your ears. The first line gives the strongest impression, and the last line gives the second strongest impression. We can use this psychological phenomenon to give our choruses increased impact.

A chorus can be said to be comprised of lines and hooks (or "titles").

- A *line* is generally the lyrics over eight beats (two measures), or whatever the phrase structure is of your song. Of course, this is a simplification. But choruses are most commonly four lines, over eight measures, and we will base this lesson on that type of structure.
- A *hook* is the song's most memorable line. Often, this includes the song title, and so the terms "hook" and "title" are commonly used interchangeably, though many song titles actually do not actually occur in the song's lyrics (e.g., "Bohemian Rhapsody" by Queen). And the term "hook" is also used to mean memorable instrumental figures. In lyric notation, we will use T to indicate a title/hook line.
- A *swing line* is a line in the chorus that is not the hook. In lyric notation, we will use a tilde (~) to indicate a swing line.

Understanding that the opening line of a chorus gives a title/hook the most prominent placement, and that the last line is the second most prominent placement, gives us a tremendous opportunity to create prosody in our choruses, helping us control the level of emotional impact the title/hook placement has on the lyric story. There are various patterns of titles and swing lines in choruses, and each has a unique impact. We will look at some of the most effective.

SINGLE T LINE PLACEMENT

In the first group of chorus types, the title/hook occurs just once.

~~~T

One of the most common chorus forms is putting the title/hook in the last line: ~~~T. Here, the swing lines set up or lead to the last important line.

You could use this form to show somebody that overcame something at the end, or didn't realize something until too late, or waited too long to make a choice, or things turned out okay, or maybe the character is a punchline (which comes at the end of a joke) in a relationship, or maybe they are at the bottom of a problem. Or imagine you are writing a song about a character being shy. Maybe putting a title about being shy at the end of the chorus shows just how introverted they are—like they are hiding behind all the other lines.

Some examples:

- "Everybody Talks" by Neon Trees. The chorus is about how a rumor takes shape. It starts with a whisper and ends up with everyone talking. Well guess where the title is? Yes...at the end, when everybody is talking. Isn't that brilliant?
- "Better Dig Two" by the Band Perry. A fantastic two-line version of this form (~T), especially if you think of the grave as being a final resting place.
- "Barracuda" by Heart is also terrific, as the "barracuda" is someone hiding in the bottom of the weeds.

T~~~

In a T~~~ chorus structure, the opening position gives your title tremendous impact. You can use this form to show power. Remember our shy person in the last chorus form? What if they decided today's the day to confess their undying love for someone? Or what if it is about always being the first one hurt in a relationship, or the first to leave, or the first to fall in love, or having one barrier or obstacle to what you want/need. Maybe the lyric is about the one thing holding everything else together, or the start of a new relationship, or new phase of life?

- "Royals" by Lorde is about someone poor in a world of wealth. In the chorus, the title "Royals" occurs in the opening line—like people who are royal/rich are at the front of everything, and at the forefront of her fantasy life. This reflects the song's idea that while we will never be like them, it is still the most important thing we want.
- "Candle in the Wind" by Elton John uses this form to depict Marilyn Monroe as a singular figure who was lost suddenly.

~T~~ and ~~T~

Setting the title/hook in line 2 or 3 is uncommon, but you can still consider what impact each has. "Africa" by Toto and "Blurred Lines" by Robin Thicke use these forms.

DOUBLE T LINE OPTIONS

~T~T

Notice this chorus form's back-and-forth interplay. What if you used it for a lyric about an argument? Does having the title on the end mean you won or got the last word? Or what if the lyric was about a couple constantly breaking up but in the end find themselves together? How about a broken heart finally healed? This form could represent a lyric about being confused but finally coming to a solution?

- In "Shake It Off" by Taylor Swift, the back-and-forth of lines 1 and 3 draws attention to the way the narrator is constantly mistreated, and lines 2 and 4 literally "shake off" that mistreatment.
- In "Counting Stars" by One Republic, consider the title "counting stars" in relation to its chorus form. Imagine the swing lines are the person looking up at the sky, and the Ts being the stars the narrator finds. The swing lines are about losing sleep and dreaming, and the title lines are about action: praying and counting stars.

T~T~

More back and forth with this chorus form, but with a stronger opening and weaker ending. Maybe the argument of this lyric is left unresolved? Maybe an important search or inquiry leads nowhere? A debilitating bad habit is finally overcome, or vanquishing a reoccurring mental or physical adversity? A promise constantly being broken would fit well here. Or perhaps an old wound reopened.

"Wrecking Ball" by Miley Cyrus is a standout chorus using this form, imagine a wrecking ball swinging over and over into a wall until it crashes down!

T~~T

This is a powerful chorus form. It utilizes the title/hook in *both* the opening and closing lines. This could represent a lyric about a long-distance relationship, or maybe two people that have grown apart? It could be losing something important only to find it in the end. Maybe an emotional chasm is being crossed or the song lyric is about reuniting. I personally used this in a song about lovers messaging each other because the form wonderfully represents the position of thumbs texting on either side of a smartphone.

- "Bills" by LunchMoney Lewis has a chorus that uses this form to create a hole in the pocket of the narrator paying too many bills.
- In "Careless Whisper" by George Michael, the chorus exemplifies lonely consequence of cheating by putting the hook "Never Gonna Dance Again" (which is not the song's formal title!) on both ends while leaving the middle empty.

~~TT, TT~~, ~TT~

The following aren't as common, but are absolutely worth exploring.

- **~~TT.** Similar to a single line ending, this chorus form has an even stronger closure. Maybe in the lyric you're *really* done with someone... the relationship is unquestionably *o-ver*! Or what if someone came through in an unexpected way? Or maybe the narrator *finally* finds the great love of their life! Check out the Imagine Dragons song "Radioactive," which uses this form. The song's narrator wakes up in the first line (also great prosody!) and declares himself powerfully radioactive (a double dose in each last line!) by the end. Brilliant!
- **TT~~.** This could be a love that burned bright initially but quickly fizzled out, or maybe an initially bold impression that turned out different? Some examples:
    - "Babylon Sisters" by Steely Dan
    - "Beautiful" by Christina Aguilera uses this in a three-line chorus, as in: TT~
    - "Heartbreak Warfare" by John Mayer
- **~TT~.** "Stuck in the Middle with You" by Stealers Wheel doesn't have a chorus, but the first verse *ends* with the title followed directly by its second verse, which *begins* with the title creating a "stuck in the middle with you" effect. It isn't really a true example of a ~TT~ chorus form, but it's similar, and I get a shot of endorphins whenever I hear that moment of the song.

TRIPLE PLACEMENT OPTIONS

Triple placements are rarer than the other forms across all genres, which means they can stand out more simply for not being the norm. Having the title/hook in a majority of lines makes a powerful statement.

- **~TTT.** This is a very sneaky chorus form, because the strongest line in the section is the only line without the title/hook. In fact, you don't know the second line is a title line until the title's repetition in the third line, which is then powerfully reinforced in the last line. This is rarely used.
- **TTT~.** This form starts as strong and stays strong only to lose grip in the final moment. We're conditioned to expect the fourth line to have a title/hook if the first three have it. It is a jolting, unexpected ending. An example is "Crazy" (Brian Burton, Chomas Callaway, Gian Franco Reverberi, Gian Piero Reverberi; performed by Gnarles Barkley).
- **T~TT.** This form has a retroactive feel to it. The first line is always powerful, but it doesn't get repetition until the third line. T~T~ is a far more common chorus form, so we tend to expect a swing line after T~T; when the title/hook returns in the last line, it gets extra emphasis. An example is "Two Tickets to Paradise" (Eddie Money).

TT~T

This is a powerful chorus form. A four-line section that starts with TT tends to feel like it will be TTTT, so the surprise swing line gets a little boost of attention before returning back to a title/hook in the end. Some examples:

- "We Are Never Ever Getting Back Together (Taylor Swift, Shellback, Max Martin; performed by Taylor Swift).
- "Shake It Out" (Florence Welch, Paul Epworth; performed by Florence and the Machine)
- "Cups (When I'm Gone)" (A.P. Carter, Luisa Gerstein, Heloise Tunstall-Behrens; performed by Anna Kendrick)

QUADRUPLE T PLACEMENT OPTIONS: TTTT

Placing your title/hook in *every* line makes it an emphatic expression. This is the equivalent of using three exclamation marks at the end of a sentence!!! I used to think this form was lazy, repetitive writing—until my research revealed that more songs, across all genres, in all decades, use this form more than all the other forms combined. I was blown away by the sheer number of *my* own favorite songs that utilize this form. Some examples:

- "Call Me" (Debbie Harry, Giorgio Moroder; performed by Blondie)
- "All About That Bass" (Meghan Trainor, Kevin Kadish; performed by Meghan Trainor)
- "Chain of Fools" (Don Covay; performed by Arethra Franklin)
- "Carwash" (Norman Whitfield; performed by Rose Royce)
- "Get Lucky" (Thomas Bangalter, Guy-Manuel de Homem-Christo, Nile Rodgers, Pharrell Williams; performed by Daft Punk)

ACTIVITY

Figure out the chorus form for all the songs on your Top 20 Songs list. How does the chorus form affect the prosody of each song's chorus? Would any of the songs benefit from a different chorus form? Are the chorus forms on your songs list similar or different? Are there any surprises?

Note: I pay attention to the chorus form on every song that I hear. It is one of the easiest analysis tools.

YOUR NEXT SONG

Pick a title from your Mozart Method exercise. Experiment setting that title with at least three or four different chorus forms. Ask yourself what emotional effect each chorus form has on the title. Choose the chorus form that you feel reveals the best prosody for that title.

CHAPTER 6

Song Mapping in 2D

Sketch out a verse outline to craft non-redundant verses.

Verses move the song's story forward, and each verse should significantly change the way a listener experiences the chorus (which contains the main theme of the song). The better the verses and chorus (or refrain line) work together, the better the song connects with listeners.

The storytelling technique of changing perspective from verse to verse creates a two-dimensional song where each verse colors the chorus or refrain differently, even if the song is not an actual "story" song. To clarify:

- One-dimensional song: All verse lyrics are similar, and the order doesn't matter. While there are some great examples (e.g., "The Hokey Pokey"), a common failing of some song drafts is that they are essentially a series of lists, with limited or no motion in the narrative, which limits their overall impact.
- Two-dimensional song: Verse lyrics approach the chorus from different perspectives but are not dependent on each other. Their order doesn't matter. For example, "YMCA" (Jacques Morali, Victor Willis; performed by the Village People).
- Three-dimensional song: Verses are different perspectives, and each subsequent verse is dependent on the preceding verse (discussed in the next chapter). For example, "You Can Sleep While I Drive" (Melissa Etheridge)

Say you're writing a love song about how good-looking your significant other is. In a 2D song, one verse could be about their eyes, another verse about their smile, and the last verse (or bridge) about their hair. Or, maybe your song is about their many good traits. Can you divide "good traits" into three different categories—say, a verse about how kind they are, a verse about how hard-working they are, and a verse (or bridge) about how funny they are?

The key is not to repeat the same type of information from verse to verse.

Usually, this 2D approach should be your minimum songwriting goal.

ACTIVITY: USING A SONG MAP

A great way to chart out what's happening in a song is to use a song map. A song map is a visual representation that helps you clarify the theme of each verse lyric and how each verse connects to the chorus (or refrain).

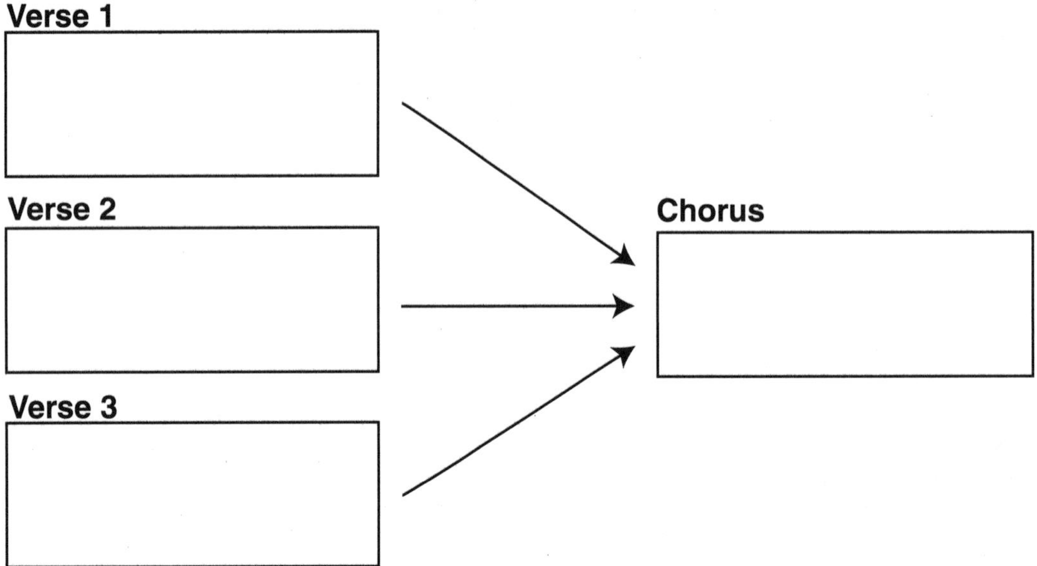

In your 2D song map, write your title/hook in the chorus block. Then, write each verse concept in a verse box. Our example has three verses, but you can use however many verses you like.

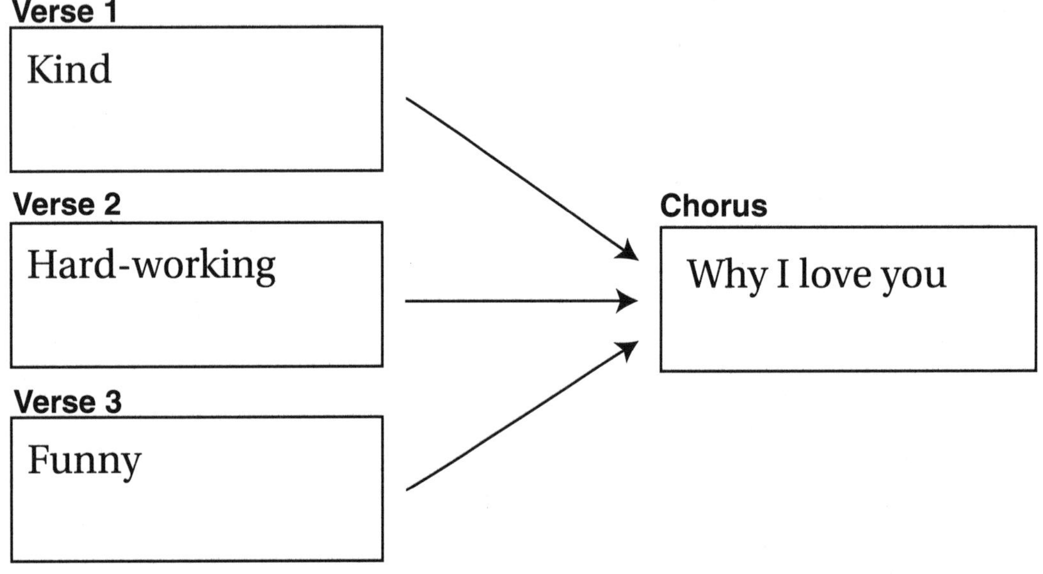

YOUR NEXT SONG

Write a song where you have mapped out the three verses and the chorus concepts before you actually write the lyrics.

CHAPTER 7

Song Mapping in 3D: But/Therefore

Engage your listeners through verses coordinated to produce and resolve conflict.

Now, we can take a song even deeper: three dimensions. In a 3D song, verses are no longer independent. Not only do they have different perspectives, but they also directly influence each other. The second verse is not just another topic, but a *result* of the first verse. The third verse (or bridge) is a *result* of the second verse. The verses of a 3D song build on each other to better magnify the chorus or refrain, creating a compelling and engaging lyric.

THE BUT/THEREFORE METHOD

This technique is called the "but/therefore" method. Once a verse idea is completed, the words "but" or "therefore" are used to brainstorm the content for subsequent verses.

- "But" creates tension, challenge, problem, or conflict to resolve between the sections—and that bit of "conflict" is central to powerful storytelling.
- "Therefore" tends to resolve the conflict.

James Taylor's song "Frozen Man" is one of my favorite examples of a 3D song lyric. His character, the fictional English sailor William James McPhee, is brought back to life after being frozen in ocean ice for a century.

- In the first verse, McPhee falls in the water and dies.
- BUT! In the second verse, he is brought back to life.
- In the bridge, he is brough back to life, BUT he is hideous and makes the children cry, and his wife and daughter are dead and gone, so he's lonely.
- *Therefore*, in the last verse, he says that the next time he dies, they shouldn't bring him back to life again. He wants to stay dead.

This evolution from verse to verse is what makes the song three dimensional.

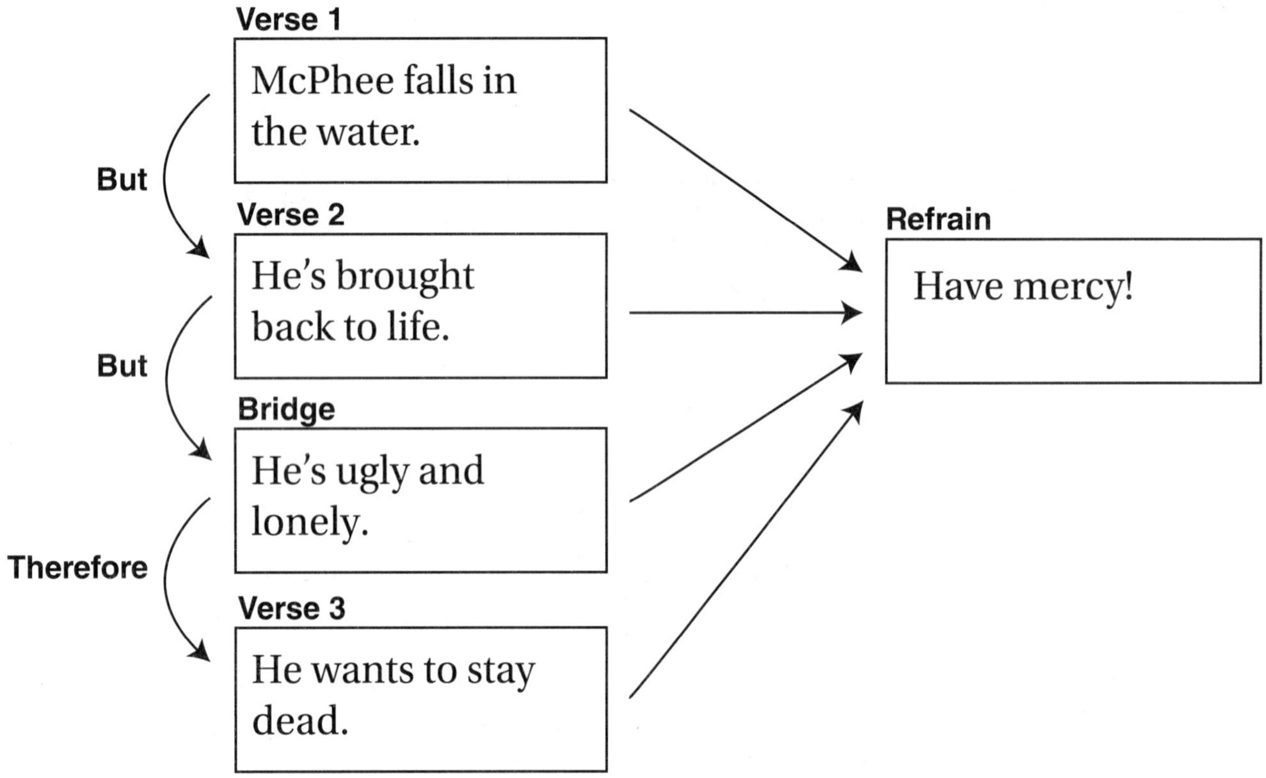

ACTIVITY: SONG MAPPING IN 3D

Return to your song map, or start a new one. Start with a verse 1 idea, but this time, use the "but/therefore" method to determine the concepts for subsequent verses.

YOUR NEXT SONG

Write a song using the song map you just created.

CHAPTER 8

Connecting Emotion to the Story

Instill your song with a foundational emotional arc.

Listeners want to be engaged with your lyric and music. They want to feel connected with you and your song. So, how can you create the greatest possible connection with your listeners? The answer: Emotion.

Songwriters often begin by writing about "situations" without revealing any emotional context. But a listener doesn't know the backstory of what they hear. While situations are definitely important, listeners emotionally connect with a song by discovering how the narrator *feels* about the situation—how the situation affects or affected them, and how the situation has changed or is changing them.

The emotions of the main character can help or hinder them, can motivate them or hold them back. They can inspire, depress, overwhelm, excite, or frustrate. But let the emotions *change* your character, because it is the journey between the beginning and ending emotion that helps your listeners "feel" what you want them to feel. It's emotion that draws a listener in.

Some songs with strong emotional arcs:

- "You Can Sleep While I Drive" by Melissa Etheridge. It starts feeling trapped and restless, and ends with feeling empowered.
- "Sail On" by the Commodores. It goes from being let down by a failed relationship to being optimistic about feeling free.

So, how do we get our songs to make our listeners feel our intended emotion?

ACTIVITY: EMOTION TIMELINE

Let's build the emotion into the lyric from the very beginning. We can chart your song's progression of emotions alongside the details that support them.

There are three essential stages experienced by your narrator or primary character:

1. Their beginning emotion. How do they feel at the start of the song?
2. Their point of change, where they shift from one emotion to another. How does the point of change catalyze their emotional transformation?
3. Their ending emotion. How has the point of change left them?

Fill in the timeline, along with any details from the situations that support the emotional journey.

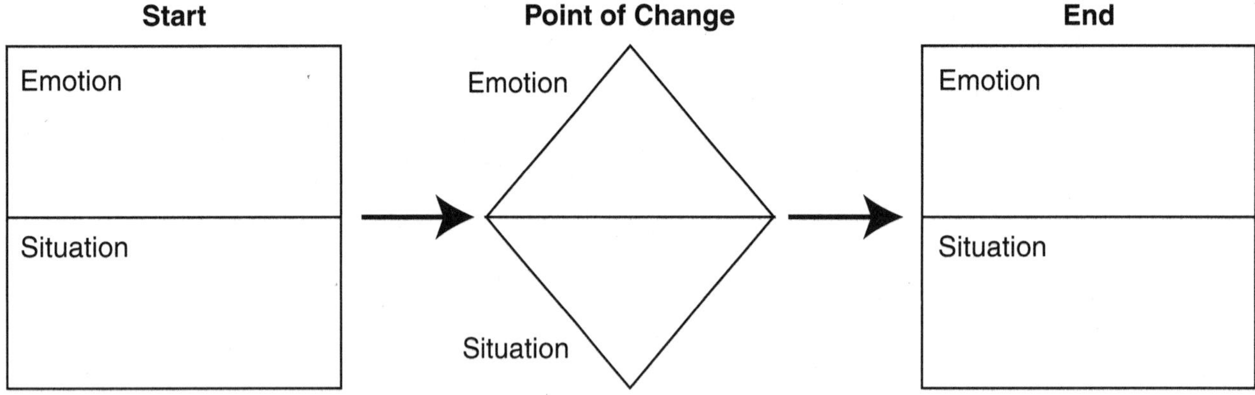

FIG. 8.1. Emotion Timeline

Note that this timeline is independent from song sections. The starting emotion can last for multiple verses, and the point of change can happen in a verse or a bridge.

Here's an example, but now mapping to a song structure.

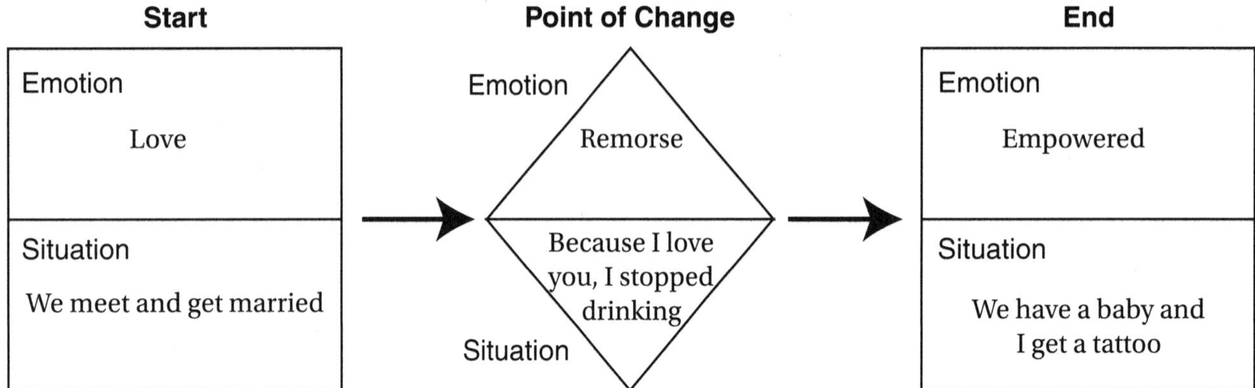

FIG. 8.2. Example Emotion Timeline

A helpful brainstorming tool in helping you articulate the specific emotions at work in you song is Uncle Shane's Emotion Chart (figure 8.3). You can even start your songwriting process by choosing random emotions from this chart, plugging them into your timeline, and then imagining stories (situations) that suit that arc.

Great songs live at a powerful new level when they tell a story in a way that helps people feel.

YOUR NEXT SONG

Write a new song by first creating an emotion timeline, then filling in the rough situations, and then finally developing lyrics and song sections to support its emotional evolution. Remember that the emotion timeline does not have to map directly to any specific song sections.

Uncle Shane's Emotion Chart

Love	Happy	Sad	Angry	Surprised	Fearful	Bad	Disgusted
Admire	Accepted	Abandoned	Aggressive	Amazed	Anxious	Apathetic	Appalled
Adulation	Aroused	Ashamed	Annoyed	Astonished	Excluded	Bored	Awful
Affection	Cheeky	Depressed	Betrayed	Awe	Exposed	Busy	Detestable
Allegiance	Confident	Despair	Bitter	Confused	Frightened	Indifferent	Disappointed
Appreciation	Content	Embarrassed	Critical	Disillusioned	Helpless	Out of Control	Disapproving
Ardor	Courageous	Empty	Dismissive	Dismayed	Inadequate	Overwhelmed	Hesitant
Attachment	Creative	Fragile	Disrespected	Eager	Insecure	Pressured	Horrified
Cling	Curious	Grief	Distant	Energetic	Insignificant	Rushed	Judgmental
Courting	Free	Guilty	Frustrated	Excited	Nervous	Sleepy	Nauseated
Delight	Hopeful	Hurt	Furious	Perplexed	Persecuted	Stressed	Repelled
Devotion	Inquisitive	Inferior	Hostile	Shocked	Rejected	Tired	Revolted
Embrace	Inspired	Isolated	Humiliated	Startled	Scared	Unfocused	
Esteem	Interested	Lonely	Indignant		Threatened		
Exalt	Intimate	Powerless	Infuriated		Weak		
Fancy	Joyful	Remorseful	Jealous		Worried		
Favor	Loving	Victimized	Let Down		Worthless		
Fondness	Optimistic	Vulnerable	Mad				
Friendship	Peaceful		Numb				
Inclination	Playful		Provoked				
Infatuation	Powerful		Resentful				
Like	Proud		Ridiculed				
Love	Sensitive		Skeptical				
Lust	Successful		Violated				
Marvel	Thankful		Withdrawn				
Passion	Trusting						
Pleasure							
Prefer							
Recognize							
Regards							
Respect							
Revere							
Soothe							
Tenderness							
Treasure							
Tryst							
Value							
Venerate							
Woo							
Worship							
Yearning							
Zeal							

FIG. 8.3. Uncle Shane's Emotion Chart

CHAPTER 9

Tempo and Its Emotional Effect

Audition tempo choices to mold the emotional undercurrent of your lyric.

Tempo is a remarkable tool for controlling the emotional perspective of a lyric.

The baseline pace of a lyric is the average speed of a normal spoken conversation. When you move beyond "what is normal," you draw attention.

So, what if we alter that baseline speed in one direction or the other? How does the delivery of a lyric alter that lyric's meaning if it is performed *dramatically* faster or slower?

There are two ways to alter a meaning through tempo: first, through changing the actual tempo of a song, and second, utilizing longer or shorter note values for the lyric—that is, controlling the density of lyrics (number of words per measure) against whatever tempo/groove is selected.

We therefore have five options, when considering controlling a song's effect using these tools. The lyrics can be at:

- talking cadence: "You Are My Sunshine" (Doug Spivey, Marv Taylor)
- slower than talking cadence: "The First Time Ever I Saw Your Face" (Ewan Maccoll; performed by Roberta Flack)
- faster than talking cadence: "The Devil Went Down to Georgia" (Charlie Daniels, Tom Crain, "Taz" DiGregorio, Fred Edwards, Charles Hayward, James W. Marshal; performed by the Charlie Daniels Band)
- lesser density of words against tempo: "Madness" (Matt Bellamy; performed by Muse)
- greater density of words against the tempo: "Rap God" (Eminem)

To keep things simple for this lesson, we will just refer to "faster" or "slower" tempos, however you accomplish them.

Generally, faster tempos are more kinetic and exciting, and slower tempos are more contemplative and thoughtful. Review your Emotion Chart, and consider what tempos seem to best reflect each emotion, or vise-versa.

ALTERING TEMPO

Here's how this works in practice. Let's pretend we are adapting the Shakespearian tragedy of *Romeo and Juliet* to a song. Our lovebirds desire to meet clandestinely because their respective families are murderously feuding. Their convergence is triggering more violence.

What tempo would best convey your intended emotion of the lyric?

Perhaps a slower, measured, unwavering delivery imparts caution. Even slower might illustrate fear. Even slower, hesitance?

What about a speedier pace to imply nervous excitement? Even faster might introduce vulnerability. Maybe a blistering delivery showcases powerlessness and despair? Or alternatively, a rise to arms?

Experiment with tempos and the note values of your lyric's vocal delivery. What does double time in a slow tempo feel like? What do long, slow notes feel like in a fast tempo? The key is being dramatic in your changes!

ACTIVITY

Choose a song section that you already wrote, or write a new one. Practice singing it with a metronome at three different tempos. If it is a song you have been working on, choose a tempo that is at least 30 bpm slower than how you have been singing it, and also a tempo 30 bpm faster than your usual one. Or just choose three tempos, such as 80, 108, and 142 bpm.

Practice singing the section at least ten times through at each tempo, and then record a final performance of each one, leaning into the character of each speed and trying to make it "work," even if it is not what you intellectually feel is best for the song.

Wait at least a day or two, and then listen back to all three recordings. How is their effect different? Which do you prefer? Is it different than what you expected to like?

YOUR NEXT SONG

When you write your next song, purposefully choose a tempo to convey an intended emotion. Try dramatically increasing and decreasing the tempo from your normal speaking cadence, in order to best capture your intended effect.

CHAPTER 10

Rhythmic Density

Control the energy level with rhythm.

Similar to tempo, the *density* of lyrics against the tempo also creates an emotional effect. Dense, rapid-fire lyrics generate more energy and excitement, while more widely spaced lyrics can be more contemplative, giving your listener more time to understand them. With denser lyrics, the speed is the sensation; with more widely spaced out lyrics, the meaning of the words has more of a chance to break through. The level of density reflects the thought processes of the narrator.

- Song with fast density: "God Mode" (Eminem)
- Song with slow density: "I Will Always Love You" (Dolly Parton; performed by Whitney Houston)

ACTIVITY

Write a lyric line, and sing it at a conversational cadence. Then try different density options, considering how each one changes the lyric's emotional impact.

1. Start with a phrase.
2. Double up the density of the entire phrase, setting it in half the number of measures. Adjust the tempo slight, if necessary.
3. Halve the density of the entire phrase, setting it over twice the number of measures. Adjust the tempo slight, if necessary.
4. Double or halve a word or a phrase.
5. Double or halve the spaces between the words or phrases.

During the songwriting process, you will commonly modify a lyric (adding words, changing words, dropping words, repeating words) in order to create more or less density, and thus control your intended effect.

YOUR NEXT SONG

When you write your next song, purposefully choose a level of lyric density to convey your intended emotions. Choose dramatically different density levels for your verses and chorus.

CHAPTER 11

A Process for Finding Rhymes

*Find words that rhyme **and** express what you want to say.*

Using lyrics that rhyme—that sound similar— helps guide our listeners to find connections within our ideas. Listeners love hearing rhymes. Scientists can even measure the endorphin rush that results when listeners make connections through hearing lyrics that rhyme—when the sonically similar fingerprint of *this* word sounds like *that* word.

To understand rhyme, let's look at how our brain processes a word as we hear it. Remember, what matters for songwriters is how the word sounds, not how it is spelled.

All words have one or more of these three *acoustic events* (groups of sounds): the onset, nucleus, and coda.

- *onset* the sounds that occur before the primary vowel of a word
- *nucleus* the primary vowel of a word
- *coda* the sounds that occur after the primary vowel

Here are some examples.

Word	Onset	Nucleus	Coda	Notes
cat	k	a	t	
tree	tr	ee		No coda
ant		a	nt	No onset
relation	rel	a	shun	Just one element in the nucleus: the stressed syllable's vowel sound
enhance	enh	a	ns	Notice that the nucleus is not the first syllable; it is the stressed syllable

Two words that rhyme have a different onset but share the same nucleus and coda. How they *sound* is your only concern; spelling has no bearing. For example, even though vowels are represented by these letters: A E I O U (and sometimes Y!), there are many more *actual* vowel sounds, which are spelled in a myriad of ways. Shoe, glue, new, goo, two, and through all represent the vowel sound oo.

HOW TO RHYME

The *nucleus*—the word's primary vowel—is the all-important starting point for a rhyme search.

Take the word "cat," which begins with a k sound (onset), followed by the "short a" (nucleus), and ends with a t sound (coda).

Word	Onset	Nucleus	Coda
cat	k	a	t

Change the onset and we have a perfect rhyme: bat, chat, fat, hat, and so on.

Words with multiple syllables are also easy to rhyme when you remember that the nucleus is always the vowel sound in the *stressed* syllable. Take the three-syllable word *relation*, each with a distinct vowel sound. The nucleus is simply the vowel in the stressed syllable: rel-*a*-shun. If we change the onset and match the nucleus/coda perfectly, we can come up with citation, deflation, creation. A good dictionary will show you how a word's syllables are stressed.

Word	Onset	Nucleus	Coda	Notes
relation	rel	a	shun	stressed syllable has the nucleus

Whenever we create a *perfect rhyme*, we are always matching two words with the same nucleus and coda but changing their onset. We will focus on perfect rhymes for now and explore other rhyme types in the next chapter.

Consonants in words can be organized into families: plosives, fricatives, nasals, vowel modifiers, and onset-only consonants. This chart shows consonant sounds of each type. We will discuss it in greater detail later in the book.

Consonant Families

Plosive		
b	d	g
p	t	k

Fricative				
v	TH	z	zh	j
f	th	s	sh	ch

Nasal		
m	n	ng

Vowel Modifier	
l	r

Onset Only	
h	w

ACTIVITY

Write a lyric line that ends in a word that has some character or flavor—your "word-to-be-rhymed."

1. Identify the onset, nucleus, and coda of your word-to-be-rhymed.
2. Use the Consonant Families chart to find potential new onset consonants. Reserve judgement for now about how much you like them. Just list all the words you can find.
3. What new words can you find if your onset sound is an actual syllable? Remember, its stress must be weaker than your currently emphasized syllable. List at least three options.

Choose at least three of the most interesting words that you have found in this process. For each one, write a lyric line leading up to it that pairs with the story of your initial line. Consider which one creates the most compelling continuation of your lyric.

YOUR NEXT SONG

Write a song section or complete song, and use the process from this lesson's activity for finding perfect rhyming words. After you write a first line of a potential rhyming couplet, list as many words as you can that rhyme perfectly with it, using this process. Then, choose the line that inspires the strongest continuation of your lyric story.

CHAPTER 12

Imperfect Rhymes

Utilize alternative rhymes to accentuate emotional connections.

While perfect rhymes vary the onset while keeping the nucleus and coda intact, *imperfect rhymes* (or "alternative rhymes") allow for changing the coda as well. Where perfect rhymes can sound clichè or too obvious, imperfect rhymes have a softer effect and can sound more natural. Using imperfect rhymes gives us many more creative options to find words that contribute to the meaning of your lyrics.

Perfect rhymes have the closest sonic connection. Each subsequent type grows slightly farther away, in terms of similarity, but they still share a special relationship with each other. Here, then, are the various types of rhyme.

Rhyme Type	Onset	Nucleus	Coda	Example
perfect	different	same	same	**cat:** bat **toss:** loss, moss **sing:** ring, wing
family	different	same	different; consonant(s) from same consonant family; any additional vowel sounds are the same	**rack:** bad, slap **huff:** love, was, plus, judge, such **mom:** gone, wrong
assonance	different	same	different; consonants from different consonant families	**hat:** jazz, can **gun:** mud, buff **truth:** boot, room
consonant	different	different	same	**win:** can, ton **slap:** rip, cop **rush:** smash, wish
additive	usually different	same	different; starts the same, but more elements than the original	**tree:** feet, least, mean, theater **hit:** mist, mister, fitted **glove:** loved, cover **blue:** dude, tomb, roost, booster
subtractive	usually different	same	different; starts the same, but fewer elements than the original	**feast:** tree, treat, peace **breathing:** teethe, free, he **wished:** dish, fit **common:** trauma, bomb

Different rhyme types can be placed in a spectrum of connection. Across the spectrum are *degrees* of strength or weakness in rhymes, and thus in connections of ideas. Pat Pattison describes this brilliantly in his book *Songwriting: Essential Guide to Rhyming* (Berklee Press).

We can exploit these different levels of connection in our writing. By choosing rhyme type, we control the relative stability or instability of our rhyme structures through choosing rhymes that have either a strong connection or different degrees of weakness.

Internal Rhymes

We have been addresing rhymes that occur at the end of phrases. Rhyming words *within* phrases are called "internal rhymes," and the abundance of imperfect rhymes are particularly useful in internal rhyming contexts. Here's an example of a lyric with internal rhyme.

*Same st***orm***, different m***orn***ing, same fur c***oat** *keeps him w***arm**

Using internal rhymes creates more connection within a line. Internal rhymes also create more momentum—similar to rhythmic density of lyrics, as discussed earlier. There is a rhythm in your rhyming patterns.

The more rhymes you have inside a line and the closer rhymes are together, the more momentum you create. Rhymes that are farther away have less momentum. Like rhythmic density, these effects uccur outside of tempo. You can make a section feel faster by increasing the amount of internal rhymes, even while the tempo remains the same.

ACTIVITY

Choose a lyric line that you want to develop into a song section. Find solutions from each one of the different rhyme types for its last word. Then build each word into a complete rhyming lyric line. Which line supports your lyric story in the most compelling way?

YOUR NEXT SONG

Write a song or song section by approaching the rhyme pattern by first considering different rhyme types, choosing rhyming words that best tell your lyric's story. Try including some internal rhymes.

CHAPTER 13

Descriptions and Metaphors/Similes

Enhance your descriptions by generating compelling connections.

When it comes to descriptions, our brain loves dramatic connections and comparisons. The more layered the connection, the more compelling the storytelling. We achieve the most interesting comparative results through the use of metaphors and similes, where something serves as a symbol for something else.

Our natural inclination is to see things as they actually are, *without* comparison: the sky is blue, razors are sharp, sugar is sweet, Shane is handsome! Are these descriptions accurate? Yes. Completely. Are they compelling? Perhaps, but often not particularly. Our brains can plow right past these accurate depictions with a meager "yep" and never think of them again.

The good news is that you can harness our natural penchant for accuracy and springboard it directly into the realm of deliciously unique metaphors and similes.

A metaphor can be an object or story, or a metaphor can be a figure of speech, implying a resemblance by using words such as *is, are, were, was*, etc.:

- That haircut is the bomb.
- You are a jewel.
- Her jokes were the cat's pajamas.
- The test was a bear.

Similes are a type of metaphor where two normally unrelated things are explicitly compared using words such as *like* and *as*:

- That racecar is *like* a rocket.
- My joke is as funny *as* a headache.

In our songwriting, when we choose words to describe an object, we can control the degree of how much we keep the focus on the object itself versus how much we keep the focus on the words that describe it—thus letting the object transcend to mean something more than it is on the surface.

- A simple description focuses on the object.
- A simile transcends the object's surface meaning but softens the effect.
- A metaphor (without like or as) lets the object transcend into something larger.

Here's a lyric with an actual description. The most basic form of description is just to say what the object is, on its surface.

His shirt is red.

This is often an effective way to present an object. Focusing directly on an object can be intimate.

To broaden the meaning, we can compare the object to something else—in this case, structured as a *simile*, a type of comparison that uses the words "like" or "as" in its construction.

His shirt is red, ***like*** *a fire engine.*

Setting the lyric as a metaphor (omitting "like") can make it more compelling.

His shirt is a red fire engine.

Changing the sequence of words can make it even more compelling:

His fire-engine red shirt...

Once we have established a metaphor, we can develop it into a larger song structure. In this example, we introduce a second idea related to fire engines: bursting (as in, bursting into flames).

He burst into our lives in his fire-engine red shirt.

Let's compare the effects of these options.

Lyric	Type	Focus
His shirt is red.	Actual Description	Focus is on the object (the shirt).
His shirt is red, like a fire engine.	Simile	Focus stays on the shirt, but it is embellished by the fire engine.
His shirt is a red fire engine	Metaphor	Focus shifts to the fire engine because it is more jarring.
He burst into our lives in his fire-engine red shirt.	Expanded Metaphor	Focus transcends from the objects to his spirit, with the shirt now serving a larger functional dimension of the song's story and emotional arc.

Metaphors/similes can be used to describe anything: emotions, people, situations, locations, etc. Trying different options for how they focus can bring extra dimension to your lyric story.

ACTIVITY

Try these steps to creating a compelling metaphor/simile.

Step 1. Determine the thing you want to describe. This can be an object, an emotion, etc.

Step 2. Write down the first characteristic(s) that come to mind regarding the thing you want to describe. I love going with first impressions here, even when my first impressions seem boring or too specific. Those "accurate" characteristics may turn into amazing descriptions.

Step 3. Consider the first characteristics you identified, and then write down the first thing that comes to mind that shares these attributes.

Step 4. Connect the original Step 1 Thing with the Step 3 Thing to create a metaphor/simile.

This results in a single metaphor/simile that may or may not be good enough to use in your song. The next two steps can help tweak your results into something more fruitful.

Step 5. Find additional characteristics that are *inherent* to the Step 3 Thing, but are *unrelated* to the Step 1 Thing.

Step 6. Use those unrelated characteristics to bolster your metaphor/simile.

These songs have a simile/metaphor in their title:

- Simile: "Body Like a Back Road" (Zach Crowell, Shane McAnally, Josh Osborne; performed by Sam Hunt)
- Simile: "She's Like the Wind" (Patrick Swayze, Stacy Widelitz; performed by Patrick Swayze
- Simile: "Vagabond" (Shane Adams)
- Metaphor: "Your Body Is a Wonderland" (John Mayer)
- Metaphor: "Ain't No Sunshine" (Bill Withers)

Let's try a real-world example, where you can practice the steps while examining my own process in using this approach. I had the sad honor to write and perform a song ("Vagabond") at a memorial of a dear nephew, who tragically passed away. As he became an adult, we drifted apart, but his loss was still heartbreaking. In writing the lyrics, I desired to represent his life honestly, but without being trite, and therefore wanted to use a metaphor/simile in my lyrics.

Step 1. Determine the *thing* you want to describe.

The thing I wanted to describe: his life (and, if lucky, the impact of his loss).

Step 2. Write down the first characteristic(s) that come to mind regarding the thing you want to describe.

He lived a somewhat tumultuous life and struggled with personal issues, but was also a deep thinker and artistically minded.

The first characteristics that came to my mind regarding his life:

- tumultuous
- ongoing struggles
- deep thinker
- artistic

Step 3. Consider the first characteristics you identified, and then write down the first thing that comes to mind that shares these attributes.

I remembered he loved comic books, specifically the Marvel universe. Perfect! Comic books are artistic stories full of struggles, and I got a wonderful double meaning for the word "issues."

Step 4. Connect the original Step 1 Thing with the Step 3 Thing to create a metaphor/simile.

- Step 1 Thing: His life
- Step 3 Thing: Comic books

Which become:

- Metaphor: His life *was* a comic book.
- Simile: His life was *like* a comic book.

For the actual song, I chose to use the simile version, as it felt "softer."

Step 5. Find additional characteristics that are *inherent* to the Step 3 Thing, but are *unrelated* to the Step 1 Thing.

- Comic books are stories.
- Comic books have pages.
- Comic books have panels.
- Comic books feature heroes battling threats/monsters.
- Comic books are colorful.
- The hero wins in the end.*

* When I thought of this characteristic, I knew I could subvert it to create something special in the lyric.

Step 6. Use those unrelated characteristics to bolster your metaphor/simile.

Here's how the verse turned out:

Your story's like your comic books, every issue, every panel
A hero and his demons locked in epic battle
But on the final pages, the hero isn't here
And I'm the one left fighting...fighting back my tears

One of the beautiful things of this method is that in steps 5 and 6, because of your unique perspective of how you see and experience the world, your metaphors/similes become deeply personal.

YOUR NEXT SONG

Write a song section based on an interesting metaphor for a feeling or emotion.

CHAPTER 14

Word Stress Matching Between Sections

Create a tighter second verse.

When a song's verses all share the same patterns of stressed words in each lyric line, they seem more intentional, and are therefore more impactful and memorable. When later verses don't match, they comes across as unintentional and disjointed, and are less memorable for your listener.

This matching of stressed patterns can either be *perfect* (with an identical amount of stressed/unstressed syllables, in identical positions) or *imperfect* (with the same number of stressed syllables, regardless of the amount of unstressed syllables). Perfect matching is perhaps ideal, but can feel restrictive. Using imperfect matches can give you tremendous additional creative freedom.

Perfect (four stresses):

Stay**, to **wish** is to **whis**per your **name
Stay**, to **leave** and to **die** is the **same

Imperfect (five stresses):

Stay**, the **moon climbs** a **rusty sky
Stay**, I **fool**ishly **lost track** of **time

ACTIVITY

Select one of your Top 20 Songs that has multiple verses, and analyze the stress patterns between verses. Do the verses match each other perfectly, imperfectly, or not at all?

YOUR NEXT SONG

Write a verse to a new song. Then write the song's second verse, matching the second verse's rhythmic stress patterns to the first verse, either perfectly or imperfectly.

CHAPTER 15

Committing to a Point of View

Audition different narrator perspectives to create varying degrees of intimacy between you and your listener.

Different narrator perspectives create varying degrees of intimacy between a song's narrator and its listener. I like to try various perspective approaches to determine which best fits the story and has the most emotional impact.

There are two dimensions to think about when crafting the song's perspective: the narrator's (i.e., singer's) perspective, and then who the narrator is addressing and whether that person features in the narrative.

These are the three narrative perspectives:

- First person: I, me, my, we. Narrator is a character in the narrative. As first person, the narrator can address you, he/she, or me.

  I was a bouncer in a cocktail bar

- Second person: You. The listener is a character in the narrative; the narrator is not. The narrator can address you, he/him, she/her, but not me.

  You were a bouncer in a cocktail bar

- Third person: Him, her, he, she, it, they, (names). The narrator and listener are not part of the narrative; it is about others.

  Sue was a bouncer in a cocktail bar

HOW TO USE PERSPECTIVE

When you are crafting or choosing a narrative perspective, consider these three dimensions and their effect.

- **Consistency.** Usually, the narrative perspective is the same throughout the song. Mixing up different points of view tends to make the song feel disjointed. If there's no benefit to doing that (and it is rare that there is), it's best to keep the perspective consistent.

- **Level of intimacy.** Different perspectives lend the song varying degrees of intimacy.
    - *First person* is intimate and confessional. For example, "Can't Help Falling in Love" (Hugo Peretti, Luigi Creatore, George David Weiss; performed by Elvis Presley)
    - *Second person* can be intimate, but potentially more confrontational than first person. For example, "Dancing Queen" (Benny Andersson, Björn Ulvaeus, Stig Anderson; performed by ABBA)
    - *Third person* is a relatively detached storytelling approach. This is the realm of a traditional story song. The focus here is on the story itself, without the potential distraction of the narrator or listener being in the story. For example, "99 Red Balloons" (Uwe Fahrenkrog-Petersen, Kevin McAlea; performed by Nena)
- **Plausibility of communication style.** Does the approach seem like a natural way for characters to communicate with each other?

ACTIVITY

Choose several songs from your song list, and identify each one's narrative perspective. How does this affect the song's feeling of intimacy? Does changing the perspective make it better or worse?

YOUR NEXT SONG

Write a multi-verse song, or choose one that you have already mostly completed. Make sure your narrative perspective remains consistent between all the verses. Then create new variations of the song from each narrative perspective. How does each version affect the song's feeling of intimacy?

CHAPTER 16

Possessive Pronouns

Make a lyric more personal and intimate using possessive pronouns.

Within the overall narrative perspective of a song, there can be smaller-scale decisions for making individual lyrics more or less intimate by using personal pronouns. Replacing articles like *a, the,* and *this/that* with possessive pronouns like *your, my, our, her,* and *his* makes that possessed object seem more important than other objects in the narrative—and gives that lyric a more intimate effect.

Original (articles)	Modified (possessive pronouns)
The heart wants what it wants.	*My* heart wants what it wants.
A passing glance caught me by surprise.	*Her* passing glance caught me by surprise.
That attitude is abrasive.	*Your* attitude is abrasive.
I drove to school.	I drove to *our* school.

This added focus might be exactly what you want for your narrative, or it might cause a detail to take on more importance than what the story warrants. The goal is to control an object's prominence within your overall narrative. Also try possessive proper nouns, like changing "The dog is offended" to "Scarlet's dog is offended."

ACTIVITY

Choose several songs from your "Favorites" list, and look for mentions of objects, places, and emotions. Are they preceded by articles or possessive pronouns? What is the effect of changing these words from one type to the other?

YOUR NEXT SONG

Write a lyric and consider which objects and emotions should be possessed by one of the characters of your song. Look for objects, places, and emotions preceded by *a, the, that,* and *this.*

Part II

Harmony

In the next part of the book, we will explore ways to push the boundaries of how chords contribute to and support the emotional intent of a song. We'll look at new and interesting color combinations, how to manipulate a song's momentum through chord placement, how to create fresh chord progressions by repurposing and reordering chord progressions, and some other fun tricks and techniques. Let's get to it!

CHAPTER 17

Harmonic Rhythm and Momentum

Use harmonic rhythm to control the perceived momentum of a composition.

One of my favorite ways to play with chords in a song is to alter how often one chord changes to a new chord. This is called *harmonic rhythm*, and it creates some wonderful potential for prosody. Let's first talk about the mechanics of harmonic rhythm and then discuss some creative applications.

There are two types of harmonic rhythm: symmetric and asymmetric.

- *Symmetric* harmonic rhythm is where the chords are equidistant. They change from one to the next in equal components of time.
- *Asymmetric* harmonic rhythm is where the chords are non-equidistant; they are not equally spaced.

Let's take a common chord progression, G C Emin D, and play with its symmetry.

It is common for most songs to have four musical "lines" in each section, with each of those lines consisting of eight beats, and those eight beats divided over two measures. Something like this:

<table>
<tr><td></td><td colspan="32">Verse</td></tr>
<tr><td>Lines</td><td colspan="8">1</td><td colspan="8">2</td><td colspan="8">3</td><td colspan="8">4</td></tr>
<tr><td>Measures</td><td colspan="4">1</td><td colspan="4">2</td><td colspan="4">3</td><td colspan="4">4</td><td colspan="4">5</td><td colspan="4">6</td><td colspan="4">7</td><td colspan="4">8</td></tr>
<tr><td>Beats</td><td></td><td></td><td></td><td></td><td></td><td></td><td></td><td></td><td></td><td></td><td></td><td></td><td></td><td></td><td></td><td></td><td></td><td></td><td></td><td></td><td></td><td></td><td></td><td></td><td></td><td></td><td></td><td></td><td></td><td></td><td></td><td></td></tr>
</table>

SYMMETRIC HARMONIC RHYTHM

The most common harmonic rhythm is to have a new chord every two beats, so our chord progression would look like this:

	One Lyric Line							
Measure	1				2			
Chords	G		C		Emin		D	
Beats	1.1	1.2	1.3	1.4	2.1	2.2	2.3	2.4

We can increase this harmonic rhythm to one chord per beat. Notice that this harmonic rhythm "feels" faster, even though we are using the same chords at the same tempo.

	One Lyric Line							
Measure	1				2			
Chords	G	C	Emin	D	G	C	Emin	D
Beats	1.1	1.2	1.3	1.4	2.1	2.2	2.3	2.4

Now decrease the harmonic rhythm to one chord every four beats. Notice that the progression feels slower.

	Lyric Line 1							
Measure	1				2			
Chords	G				C			
Beats	1.1	1.2	1.3	1.4	2.1	2.2	2.3	2.4
	Lyric Line 2							
Measure	3				4			
Chords	Emin				D			
Beats	3.1	3.2	3.3	3.4	4.1	4.2	4.3	4.4

Let's decrease the harmonic rhythm again to one chord per eight beats. This feels even slower.

	Lyric Line 1: Measures 1 and 2							
Chords	G							
Beats	1.1	1.2	1.3	1.4	2.1	2.2	2.3	2.4
	Lyric Line 2: Measures 3 and 4							
Chords	C							
Beats	3.1	3.2	3.3	3.4	4.1	4.2	4.3	4.4
	Lyric Line 3: Measures 5 and 6							
Chords	Emin							
Beats	5.1	5.2	5.3	5.4	6.1	6.2	6.3	6.4
	Lyric Line 4: Measures 7 and 8							
Chords	D							
Beats	7.1	7.2	7.3	7.4	8.1	8.2	8.3	8.4

These feelings of "fast" or "slow" are what I call *perceived momentum*. Notice that in all the examples, the actual chord progression is the same, it is the feeling of time that is changing. A line of a song with a faster harmonic rhythm feels faster; when you start changing chords further apart, the momentum feels slower. Again, this is completely independent of the actual tempo.

ASYMMETRIC HARMONIC RHYTHM

Asymmetric harmonic rhythms are not bound by evenly placed chords. There are no rules. For example, let's put three chords in the first measure and leave one chord in the second measure.

	One Lyric Line							
Measure	1				2			
Chords	G	C	Emin		D			
Beats	1.1	1.2	1.3	1.4	2.1	2.2	2.3	2.4

Let's try the opposite: a measure with one chord, followed by a measure with the three remaining chords.

	One Lyric Line							
Measure	1				2			
Chords	G				C	Emin	D	
Beats	1.1	1.2	1.3	1.4	2.1	2.2	2.3	2.4

How about one chord for three beats, and one chord on the fourth beat:

	One Lyric Line							
Measure	1				2			
Chords	G			C	Emin			D
Beats	1.1	1.2	1.3	1.4	2.1	2.2	2.3	2.4

...or vice versa:

	One Lyric Line							
Measure	1				2			
Chords	G	C			Emin	D		
Beats	1.1	1.2	1.3	1.4	2.1	2.2	2.3	2.4

Or combine those two:

	One Lyric Line							
Measure	1				2			
Chords	G			C	Emin	D		
Beats	1.1	1.2	1.3	1.4	2.1	2.2	2.3	2.4

These are just examples. You can put the chords as close together or as far apart as you want throughout a section. In our examples, we are setting the chords on the downbeats, but the chords can also begin on the off-beats (as anticipations and/or delays).

Here's one more example: a twelve-bar blues chord progression that increases in harmonic rhythm:

Line 1:	C7			
Line 2:	F7		C7	
Line 3:	G7	F7	C7	G7

Some examples of songs that are based on each of the different types of harmonic rhythm approach:

Symmetric Harmonic Rhythms	Asymmetric Harmonic Rhythms	Mix (Verse: Symmetric, Chorus: Asymmetric)
• "Blank Space" (Taylor Swift) • "Shape of You" (Ed Sheeran, John McDaid, Steven McCutcheon; performed by Ed Sheeran) • "Virtual Insanity" (Jay Kay, Toby Smith, Stuart Zender, Derrick McKenzie, Wallis Buchanan; performed by Jamiroquai) • "Wide Awake" (Katy Perry, Max Martin, Lukasz Gottwald, Bonnie McKee; performed by Katy Perry)	• "Still Haven't Found What I'm Looking For" (Bono, the Edge, Adam Clayton, Larry Mullen Jr.; performed by U2) • "Jump" (David Lee Roth, Eddie Van Halen, Michael Anthony, Alex Van Halen; performed by Van Halen) • "Body Like a Back Road" (Sam Hunt, Zach Crowell, Shane McAnally; performed by Sam Hunt) • "Single Ladies" (Christopher Stewart, Terius Nash, Beyoncé Knowles, Thaddis Harrel; performed by Beyoncé)	• "Kiss Me" (Matt Slocum; performed by Sixpence None the Richer) • "Hey Soul Sister" (Patrick Monahan; performed by Train) • "Everybody Talks" (Tyler Glenn; performed by Neon Trees) • "Slow Hands" (Niall Horan, Jamie Scott, John Ryan; performed by Niall Horan)

ACTIVITY

In your Top 20 Songs list, identify the harmonic rhythm of some of your favorite songs. Does the harmonic rhythm change (or not change) between sections? Does it change or not change within a section? How does the change or lack of change add to the prosody of the song? Does a change in harmonic rhythm increase or decrease momentum, particularly when leading into the chorus? Remember that you can use these techniques in your own songs.

YOUR NEXT SONG

Choose a chord progression from one of your Top 20 songs and alter its harmonic rhythm to create a new sounding progression for your next song. Try changing a symmetric harmonic rhythm to asymmetric, or vice versa. Keep in mind the opportunity of using momentum to create prosody.

CHAPTER 18

Modes and Chords

Exploit the power of harmonic light and darkness using characteristic chords of the modes.

When I have out-of-town guests visit me in Nashville, I always take them to Jack's BBQ (with its neon sign of white-winged flying pink pigs!). Jack's boasts a table of possible BBQ sauces. Do you like sweet? Hot? Sour? Tomato-based? Vinegar based? Etc. Each sauce complements your meal from a unique perspective by injecting its own personality into the original flavor.

Modes work the same way for your lyrics. Modes are variations of scales—most commonly, of the major scale. Your note choices will help flavor/intensify the meaning of your lyrics.

We are used to hearing music in the Ionian mode (what most people call the "major scale") and Aeolian mode (the natural minor scale), even though you might not have known that they were called that.

By altering a single note of either the major or minor scale, we can create different moods of each that are fresh to our ears. For example, by lowering the 7 of the major scale to ♭7, we create the Mixolydian mode. If we raise the 4 of the major scale to ♯4, we create the Lydian mode. For minor keys, if we raise the ♭6 of Aeolian to a natural 6, we arrive at Dorian. If we lower the 2 of Aeolian to ♭2, we arrive at Phrygian.

Certain genres of music tend to land in certain modes. R&B is often in Dorian; rock is often in Mixolydian. So you might already be writing in different modes without knowing the theoretical name for them.

If you try the same lyrics under different modes, their meaning will change due to the flavor introduced by that chosen mode.

The simplest way of using modes to change the effect of your lyrics is to change from a major key to a minor key (as in Ionian mode to Aeolian mode), or from minor to major. This is typically done to make a happy song sad or a sad song happy—to make your song musically either darker or lighter. There are three major modes and three minor modes typically used, all with varying degrees of dark and light to incorporate into your song. Instead of just going from major to minor, you can try going between any of the three major or minor modes

To capture the full strength and character of a mode, follow Shane's Rules for Modal Writing:

1. Establish the tonal center of the song by using the *tonic chord*—the first chord of the key (the "1" chord).
2. Establish the "flavor" of the mode by using one or more of the characteristic chords in that mode.

MODES

To describe a mode's notes, we can use either Roman numerals or regular numbers (Nashville number system). While the notes will change for different keys (tonal centers), the numerals/numbers stay the same, relative to the tonic.

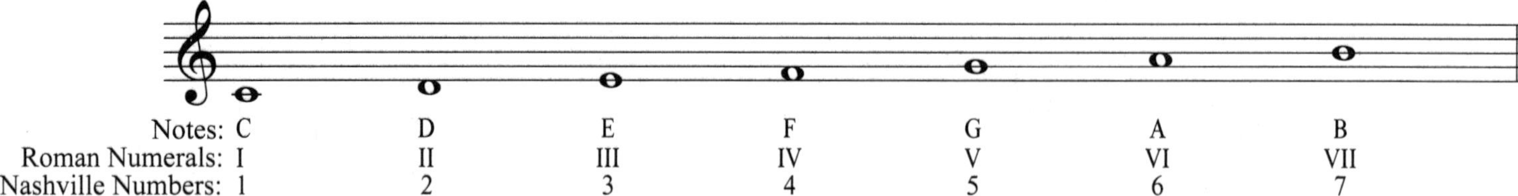

The next chart shows the seven standard modes of C major (Ionian), ordering them by brightness levels (determined by how many flatted notes each contains in relation to the major scale/Ionian mode). The gray boxes show the characteristic chords in each mode—the chords that makes the mode feel distinctive.

When you are writing a song, think about how relatively light or dark you want to color the music. Typically, you want the music and the lyric story to both be similar levels of lightness/darkness. In some styles, such as bluegrass, it is a common convention to switch them: relatively light music for darker subjects, and vice versa.

	Mode	Character	Alterations	I	II	III	IV	V	VI	VII
Major	Lydian	Bright	Sharp 4	C	**D**	Emin	F♯dim	G	Amin	**Bmin**
				CMaj7	**D7**	Emin7	F♯min7♭5	**GMaj7**	Amin7	**Bmin7**
	Ionian	Neutral	(none)	C	Dmin	Emin	F	G	Amin	Bdim
				CMaj7	Dmin7	Emin7	FMaj7	**G7**	Amin7	B7min7♭5
	Mixolydian	Less Bright	Flat 7	C	Dmin	Edim	F	**Gmin**	Amin	**B♭**
				C7	Dmin7	Emin7♭5	FMaj7	**Gmin7**	Amin7	**B♭Maj7**
Minor	Dorian	Dark	Flat 3, 7	Cmin	**Dmin**	E♭	**F**	Gmin	Adim	**B♭**
				Cmin7	**Dmin7**	E♭Maj7	**F7**	Gmin7	Amin7♭5	**B♭Maj7**
	Aeolian	Darker	Flat 3, 6, 7	Cmin	Ddim	E♭	**Fmin**	Gmin	**A♭**	B♭
				Cmin7	Dmin7♭5	E♭Maj7	**Fmin7**	Gmin7	**A♭Maj7**	**B♭7**
	Phrygian	Darkest	Flat 2, 3, 6, 7	Cmin	**D♭**	E♭	Fmin	Gdim	A♭	**B♭min**
				Cmin7	**D♭Maj7**	**E♭7**	Fmin7	Gmin7♭5	A♭Maj7	**B♭min7**
	Locrian	(not typically used)	Flat 2, 3, 5, 6, 7	Cdim	D♭	E♭min	Fmin	G♭	A♭	B♭min
				Cmin7♭5	D♭Maj7	E♭min7	Fmin7	G♭Maj7	A♭7	B♭min7

Notes:

1. The Ionian mode is more commonly called "the major scale" (and is the most commonly used major mode).
2. The Aeolian mode is commonly called "the natural minor scale" (and is the most commonly used minor mode).
3. Lydian, Ionian, and Mixolydian are considered major modes because their I chord is major.
4. Dorian, Aeolian, and Phrygian are considered minor modes because their I chord is minor.
5. The Locrian mode is so dissonant that it is usually considered unusable.

Characteristic Chords in Each Mode (All Keys)

Lydian

IMaj7	II7	IIImin7	♯IVmin7♭5	VMaj7	VImin7	VIImin7
AMaj7	B7	C♯min7	D♯min7♭5	EMaj7	F♯min7	G♯min7
BMaj7	C♯7	D♯min7	E♯min7♭5	F♯Maj7	G♯min7	A♯min7
CMaj7	D7	Emin7	F♯min7♭5	GMaj7	Amin7	Bmin7
DMaj7	E7	F♯min7	G♯min7♭5	AMaj7	Bmin7	C♯min7
EMaj7	F♯7	G♯min7	A♯min7♭5	BMaj7	C♯min7	D♯min7
FMaj7	G7	Amin7	Bmin7♭5	CMaj7	Dmin7	Emin7
GMaj7	A7	Bmin7	C♯min7♭5	DMaj7	Emin7	F♯min7
A♭Maj7	B♭7	Cmin7	Dmin7♭5	E♭Maj7	Fmin7	Gmin7
B♭Maj7	C7	Dmin7	Emin7♭5	FMaj7	Gmin7	Amin7
C♭Maj7	D♭7	E♭min7	Fmin7♭5	G♭Maj7	A♭min7	B♭min7
D♭Maj7	E♭7	Fmin7	Gmin7♭5	A♭Maj7	B♭min7	Cmin7
E♭Maj7	F7	Gmin7	Amin7♭5	B♭Maj7	Cmin7	Dmin7
G♭Maj7	A♭7	B♭min7	Cmin7♭5	D♭Maj7	E♭min7	Fmin7
C♯Maj7	D♯7	E♯min7	F♯♯min7♭5	G♯Maj7	A♯min7	B♯min7
F♯Maj7	G♯7	A♯min7	B♯min7♭5	C♯Maj7	D♯min7	E♯min7

Dorian

Imin7	IImin7	♭IIIMaj7	IV7	Vmin7	VImin7♭5	♭VIIMaj7
Amin7	Bmin7	CMaj7	D7	Emin7	F♯min7♭5	GMaj7
Bmin7	C♯min7	DMaj7	E7	F♯min7	G♯min7♭5	AMaj7
Cmin7	Dmin7	E♭Maj7	F7	Gmin7	Amin7♭5	B♭Maj7
Dmin7	Emin7	FMaj7	G7	Amin7	Bmin7♭5	CMaj7
Emin7	F♯min7	GMaj7	A7	Bmin7	C♯min7♭5	DMaj7
Fmin7	Gmin7	A♭Maj7	B♭7	Cmin7	Dmin7♭5	E♭Maj7
Gmin7	Amin7	B♭Maj7	C7	Dmin7	Emin7♭5	FMaj7
A♭min7	B♭min7	C♭Maj7	D♭7	E♭min7	Fmin7♭5	G♭Maj7
B♭min7	Cmin7	D♭Maj7	E♭7	Fmin7	Gmin7♭5	A♭Maj7
C♭min7	D♭min7	E♭♭Maj7	F♭7	G♭min7	A♭min7♭5	B♭♭Maj7
D♭min7	E♭min7	F♭Maj7	G♭7	A♭min7	B♭min7♭5	C♭Maj7
E♭min7	Fmin7	G♭Maj7	A♭7	B♭min7	Cmin7♭5	D♭Maj7
G♭min7	A♭min7	B♭♭Maj7	C♭7	D♭min7	E♭min7♭5	F♭Maj7
C♯min7	D♯min7	EMaj7	F♯7	G♯min7	A♯min7♭5	BMaj7
F♯min7	G♯min7	AMaj7	B7	C♯min7	D♯min7♭5	EMaj7

Ionian

Imaj7	IImin7	IIImin7	IVmaj7	V7	VImin7	VIImin7♭5
AMaj7	Bmin7	C♯min7	DMaj7	E7	F♯min7	G♯min7♭5
BMaj7	C♯min7	D♯min7	EMaj7	F♯7	G♯min7	A♯min7♭5
CMaj7	Dmin7	Emin7	FMaj7	G7	Amin7	Bmin7♭5
DMaj7	Emin7	F♯min7	GMaj7	A7	Bmin7	C♯min7♭5
EMaj7	F♯min7	G♯min7	AMaj7	B7	C♯min7	D♯min7♭5
FMaj7	Gmin7	Amin7	B♭Maj7	C7	Dmin7	Emin7♭5
GMaj7	Amin7	Bmin7	CMaj7	D7	Emin7	F♯min7♭5
A♭Maj7	B♭min7	Cmin7	D♭Maj7	E♭7	Fmin7	Gmin7♭5
B♭Maj7	Cmin7	Dmin7	E♭Maj7	F7	Gmin7	Amin7♭5
C♭Maj7	D♭min7	E♭min7	F♭Maj7	G♭7	A♭min7	B♭min7♭5
D♭Maj7	E♭min7	Fmin7	G♭Maj7	A♭7	B♭min7	Cmin7♭5
E♭Maj7	Fmin7	Gmin7	A♭Maj7	B♭7	Cmin7	Dmin7♭5
G♭Maj7	A♭min7	B♭min7	C♭Maj7	D♭7	E♭min7	Fmin7♭5
C♯Maj7	D♯min7	E♯min7	F♯Maj7	G♯7	A♯min7	B♯min7♭5
F♯Maj7	G♯min7	A♯min7	BMaj7	C♯7	D♯min7	E♯min7♭5

Aeolian

Imin7	IImin7♭5	♭IIIMaj7	IVmin7	Vmin7	♭VIMaj7	♭VII7
Amin7	Bmin7♭5	CMaj7	Dmin7	Emin7	FMaj7	G7
Bmin7	C♯min7♭5	DMaj7	Emin7	F♯min7	GMaj7	A7
Cmin7	Dmin7♭5	E♭Maj7	Fmin7	Gmin7	A♭Maj7	B♭7
Dmin7	Emin7♭5	FMaj7	Gmin7	Amin7	B♭Maj7	C7
Emin7	F♯min7♭5	GMaj7	Amin7	Bmin7	CMaj7	D7
Fmin7	Gmin7♭5	A♭Maj7	B♭min7	Cmin7	D♭Maj7	E♭7
Gmin7	Amin7♭5	B♭Maj7	Cmin7	Dmin7	E♭Maj7	F7
A♭min7	B♭min7♭5	C♭Maj7	D♭min7	E♭min7	F♭Maj7	G♭7
B♭min7	Cmin7♭5	D♭Maj7	E♭min7	Fmin7	G♭Maj7	A♭7
C♭min7	D♭min7♭5	E♭♭Maj7	F♭min7	G♭min7	A♭♭Maj7	B♭♭7
D♭min7	E♭min7♭5	F♭Maj7	G♭min7	A♭min7	B♭♭Maj7	C♭7
E♭min7	Fmin7♭5	G♭Maj7	A♭min7	B♭min7	C♭Maj7	D♭7
G♭min7	A♭min7♭5	B♭♭Maj7	C♭min7	D♭min7	E♭♭Maj7	F♭7
C♯min7	D♯min7♭5	EMaj7	F♯min7	G♯min7	AMaj7	B7
F♯min7	G♯min7♭5	AMaj7	Bmin7	C♯min7	DMaj7	E7

Mixolydian

I7	IImin7	IIImin7♭5	IVMaj7	Vmin7	VImin7	♭VIIMaj7
A7	Bmin7	C♯min7♭5	DMaj7	Emin7	F♯min7	GMaj7
B7	C♯min7	D♯min7♭5	EMaj7	F♯min7	G♯min7	AMaj7
C7	Dmin7	Emin7♭5	FMaj7	Gmin7	Amin7	B♭Maj7
D7	Emin7	F♯min7♭5	GMaj7	Amin7	Bmin7	CMaj7
E7	F♯min7	G♯min7♭5	AMaj7	Bmin7	C♯min7	DMaj7
F7	Gmin7	Amin7♭5	B♭Maj7	Cmin7	Dmin7	E♭Maj7
G7	Amin7	Bmin7♭5	CMaj7	Dmin7	Emin7	FMaj7
A♭7	B♭min7	Cmin7♭5	D♭Maj7	E♭min7	Fmin7	G♭Maj7
B♭7	Cmin7	Dmin7♭5	E♭Maj7	Fmin7	Gmin7	A♭Maj7
C♭7	D♭min7	E♭min7♭5	F♭Maj7	G♭min7	A♭min7	B♭♭Maj7
D♭7	E♭min7	Fmin7♭5	G♭Maj7	A♭min7	B♭min7	C♭Maj7
E♭7	Fmin7	Gmin7♭5	A♭Maj7	B♭min7	Cmin7	D♭Maj7
G♭7	A♭min7	B♭min7♭5	C♭Maj7	D♭min7	E♭min7	F♭Maj7
C♯7	D♯min7	E♯min7♭5	F♯Maj7	G♯min7	A♯min7	BMaj7
F♯7	G♯min7	A♯min7♭5	BMaj7	C♯min7	D♯min7	EMaj7

Phrygian

Imin7	♭IIMaj7	♭III7	♭IVmin7	♭Vmin7♭5	♭VIMaj7	♭VIImin7
Amin7	B♭Maj7	C7	Dmin7	Emin7♭5	FMaj7	Gmin7
Bmin7	CMaj7	D7	Emin7	F♯min7♭5	GMaj7	Amin7
Cmin7	D♭Maj7	E♭7	Fmin7	Gmin7♭5	A♭Maj7	B♭min7
Dmin7	E♭Maj7	F7	Gmin7	Amin7♭5	B♭Maj7	Cmin7
Emin7	FMaj7	G7	Amin7	Bmin7♭5	CMaj7	Dmin7
Fmin7	G♭Maj7	A♭7	B♭min7	Cmin7♭5	D♭Maj7	E♭min7
Gmin7	A♭Maj7	B♭7	Cmin7	Dmin7♭5	E♭Maj7	Fmin7
A♭min7	B♭♭Maj7	C♭7	D♭min7	E♭min7♭5	F♭Maj7	G♭min7
B♭min7	C♭Maj7	D♭7	E♭min7	Fmin7♭5	G♭Maj7	A♭min7
C♭min7	D♭♭Maj7	E♭♭7	F♭min7	G♭min7♭5	A♭♭Maj7	B♭♭min7
D♭min7	E♭♭Maj7	F♭7	G♭min7	A♭min7♭5	B♭♭Maj7	C♭min7
E♭min7	F♭Maj7	G♭7	A♭min7	B♭min7♭5	C♭Maj7	D♭min7
G♭min7	A♭♭Maj7	B♭♭7	C♭min7	D♭min7♭5	E♭♭Maj7	F♭min7
C♯min7	DMaj7	E7	F♯min7	G♯min7♭5	AMaj7	Bmin7
F♯min7	GMaj7	A7	Bmin7	C♯min7♭5	DMaj7	Emin7

The previous charts show the seventh chords in all keys for each of the six modes that are commonly used in contemporary songwriting. Change the seventh chords to triads by eliminating the 7's (G7 becomes G, CMaj7 becomes C, A♭min7 becomes A♭min). You can use this as a reference until you become comfortable with mode theory.

There are other types of scales and modes worth exploring, such as harmonic minor, the blues scale, pentatonic scales, and others. You can use the same approach to explore them and their permutations.

ACTIVITY

To get accustomed to the modes, practice playing through these example progressions for each mode on your instrument, in several keys. Notice how the tonic (I) is established and how the characteristic chords flavor the progression. Try using a variety of harmonic rhythms for each progression.

Mode	Examples of Characteristic Progressions			
Lydian	I	V	II	I
	IMaj7	VMaj7	VImin7	IMaj7
Ionian	I	IV	VImin	V
	IMaj7	IImin7	IIImin7	IImin7
Mixolydian	I	IV	♭VII	I
	I	Vmin7	IImin7	I
Dorian	Imin	IV	Imin	IV
	Imin7	IImin7	♭IIIMaj7	IImin7
Aeolian	Imin	♭VI	♭VII	Imin
	Imin7	IVmin7	♭VIMaj7	Imin7
Phrygian	Imin	♭II	Imin	♭III
	Imin7	♭VIImin7	♭VIMaj7	Imin7

Practice playing common chord progressions in a variety of different modes, and consider how they feel to you. Change between minor and major chords, with or without sevenths, depending on the mode you choose. Here are some progressions you might try with a variety of modes (with and without sevenths), with just the roots indicated:

Progression 1: I IV V
Progression 2: I VI II V
Progression 3: II V I
Progression 4: I ♭VII IV

Consider how the modes make you feel and what kinds of lyric stories might suit them. Your reaction will be personal. Here are some of my own thoughts about the different modes.

- *Ionian*, or "major," is the most common mode. Any chord combination will work, as exemplified in millions of songs in every genre and style imaginable. Be careful when setting the VImin (Amin in C) in a strong position, as it can lend an unintentional minor cast to the progression. Example: "Let It Be" (John Lennon, Paul McCartney; performed by the Beatles)

- *Mixolydian* gives a song a broodier, more serious tone than Ionian. Rock music is the primary playground of Mixolydian, although many genres use it to great effect. Example: "Royals" (Lorde)
- *Dorian* has a silky, soulful, sultry sound. There can be a real vulnerability, longing, and angst in Dorian. There can also be a cheekiness and playful aspect. R&B, funk, and soul live in Dorian. Example: "Moondance" (Van Morrison)
- *Aeolian*, or "natural minor," is the most commonly heard minor mode/key. This is the mode of "sad," in its many flavors: empty, lonely, hurt, numb, withdrawn, helpless. Aeolian can also be richly thoughtful. Example: "White Flag" (Dido Armstrong, Rick Nowels, Rollo Armstrong; performed by Dido)
- *Phrygian* holds a special place in my heart. I love how intimate, intense, and fragile this underutilized mode can be. Phrygian can sound isolated, grief-ridden, powerless, horrified, appalled, humiliated, astonished, startled, threatened, and overwhelmed. Phrygian's chord combinations have an unmatched power and beauty. Although suitable for any genre that needs to go to a "next level of feels," the more intense styles such as grunge and metal (in all its iterations) tend to capitalize on the powerful tones of Phrygian the most. Example: "Gin and Juice" (Calvin Broadus, David Ruffin Jr.; performed by Snoop Dogg)
- *Lydian*. The previous modes took us down a darker path. Lydian, our other major mode, goes in the opposite direction. Lydian has an awe to it. It can feel astonished and excited; it creates an openness to new possibilities. I love its cinematic, larger-than-life feeling. Lydian flavors tend to peek up in pop and alt pop styles. Example: "Landslide" (Stephanie Nicks; performed by Fleetwood Mac)

You can vary how strict or loose to be in how closely you adhere to each mode's prescribed chords. A strict approach is purely *diatonic;* you *only* use the chords in the mode. A loose approach means you throw in one of the characteristic chords to create a momentary modal flavor. It is *non-diatonic*; chords can include notes from outside the mode. Staying strictly within the mode brings out its distinctive flavor. On the other hand, the right spice of momentarily stepping outside the mode can provide a delicious jolt and showcase a lyric.

YOUR NEXT SONG

Write a new lyric, or choose a lyric from one of the activities in this book, where you haven't written any music yet. Then, as you start to add music to your lyric, cycle through the modes to choose the one that best supports your story or theme.

Make a choice to either:

1. Clearly establish the mode early on by establishing the tonic chord and utilizing the characteristic chords quickly, or
2. Delay the sound of the mode by establishing the tonic chord and delaying the use of the characteristic chords until an important moment in the lyrics.

CHAPTER 19

Alternative Chord Finder

Use focus notes to discover colorful and unconventional chords for mundane chord progressions.

Many songwriters find themselves using the same chords and chord progressions in all their songs—even when those chords aren't the best setting for their lyric. So how can we break out of this habit? How can we think outside the box?

My method is to use what I call a *focus note*: identifying a melody or chord root that occurs on an important lyric. (A focus note can be either a chord tone or a non-chord tone.) Then, I highlight that moment with a new unconventional chord.

We can put that focus note in different chord positions, such as shown in this notation:

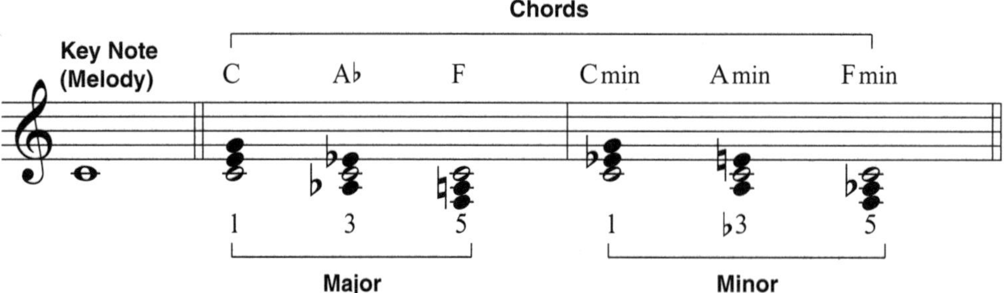

Let's say your focus note is a C, originally set on a C chord, which you would like to make more interesting. If you want to stay with a major chord in that position, you have three choices. The note C is:

- the root of a C major chord (which consists of C, E, and G)
- the 3 of an A♭ major chord (which consists of A♭, C, and E♭)
- the 5 of an F major chord (which consists of F, A, C)

Let's do the same thing with minor chords. The note C is:

- the root of a C minor chord (which consists of C, E♭, G)
- the minor 3 of an A minor chord (which consists of A, C, E)
- the 5 of an F minor chord (which consists of F, A♭, C)

In my own songwriting, I typically use eleven different chord types. These chords consist of either three or four notes.

- **Three-note chords**, with their three positions, give me fifteen possible chords to choose from…

Major Triad	1	3	5
Minor Triad	1	♭3	5
Suspended 2	1	2	5
Suspended 4	1	4	5
Minor Triad, no 5, add 11	1	♭3	11

- **Four-note chords**, with their four positions, gives me thirty-six possible chords to choose from.

Major 6	1	3	5	6
Minor chord, minor 6	1	♭3	5	♭6
Minor chord, major 6	1	♭3	5	6
Major 7	1	3	5	Maj7
Minor 7	1	♭3	5	♭7
Dominant 7	1	3	5	♭7
Minor chord, Major 7	1	♭3	5	Maj7
Add 9	1	3	5	9
Minor 7, no 5, add 11	1	♭3	11	♭7

This gives me fifty-one possible chords from a single note! Of course, you can plug your own favorite chords into these charts, and get even more results.

Initially, this many choices was overwhelming to me, so I created my "Uncle Shane's Famous Chord Finder" chart, which shows all twelve notes in a column, and then a list of possible chords to the right of each note. This enables me to quickly go down the list, and find new chords to audition in that spot.

Uncle Shane's Famous Chord Finder

	Focus Note	As Chord Root		As 2 (9)			As 3		As 4 (11)		As 5		As 6 (13)		As b7		As Maj7	
		Maj	min	Maj	min	sus2	min	Maj	add11	sus4	min	Maj	min	Maj	min	Maj	min	Maj
Natural Root	A	A	Amin	Gadd9	Gmin(add9)	Gsus2	F#min	F	Emin(add11)	Esus4	Dmin	D	Cmin6	C6	Bmin7	B7	Bbmin(Maj7)	BbMaj7
	B	B	Bmin	Aadd9	Amin(add9)	Asus2	G#min	G	F#min(add11)	F#sus4	Emin	E	Dmin6	D6	C#min7	C#7	Cmin(Maj7)	CMaj7
	C	C	Cmin	Bbadd9	Bbmin(add9)	Bbsus2	Amin	Ab	Gmin(add11)	Gsus4	Fmin	F	Ebmin6	Eb6	Dmin7	D7	Dbmin(Maj7)	DbMaj7
	D	D	Dmin	Cadd9	Cmin(add9)	Csus2	Bmin	Bb	Amin(add11)	Asus4	Gmin	G	Fmin6	F6	Emin7	E7	Ebmin(Maj7)	EbMaj7
	E	E	Emin	Dadd9	Dmin(add9)	Dsus2	Cmin	C	Bmin(add11)	Bsus4	Amin	A	Gmin6	G6	F#min7	F#7	Fmin(Maj7)	FMaj7
	F	F	Fmin	Ebadd9	Ebmin(add9)	Ebsus2	Dmin	Db	Cmin(add11)	Csus4	Bbmin	Bb	Abmin6	Ab6	Gmin7	G7	Gbmin(Maj7)	GbMaj7
	G	G	Gmin	Fadd9	Fmin(add9)	Fsus2	Emin	Eb	Dmin(add11)	Dsus4	Cmin	C	Bbmin6	Bb6	Amin7	A7	Abmin(Maj7)	AbMaj7
Flatted Root	Ab	Ab	Abmin	Gbadd9	Gbmin(add9)	Gbsus2	Fmin	E Fb	Ebmin(add11)	Ebsus4	Dbmin	Db	Cbmin6 Bmin6	Cb6 B6	Bbmin7	Bb7	Bbbmin(Maj7) Amin(Maj7)	BbbMaj7 AMaj7
	Bb	Bb	Bbmin	Abadd9	Abmin(add9)	Absus2	Gmin	Gb	Fmin(add11)	Fsus4	Ebmin	Eb	Dbmin6	Db6	Cmin7	C7	Cbmin(Maj7)	CbMaj7
	Cb	Cb	Cbmin	Aadd9	Bbbmin(add9) Amin(add9)	Bbbsus2 Asus2	Abmin	Abb G	Gbmin(add11)	Gbsus4	Fbmin Emin	Fb E	Ebbmin6 Dmin6	Ebb6 D6	Dbmin7	Db7	Dbbmin(Maj7) Cmin(Maj7)	DbbMaj7 CMaj7
	Db	Db	Dbmin	Badd9	Cbmin(add9) Bmin(add9)	Bsus2	Bbmin	Bbb A	Abmin(add11)	Absus4	Gbmin	Gb	Fbmin6 Emin6	Fb6 E6	Ebmin7	Eb7	Ebbmin(Maj7) Dmin(Maj7)	EbbMaj7 DMaj7
	Eb	Eb	Ebmin	Dbadd9	Dbmin(add9)	Dbsus2	Cmin	Cb B	Bbmin(add11)	Bbsus4	Abmin	Ab	Gbmin6	Gb6	Fmin7	F7	Fbmin(Maj7) Emin(Maj7)	FbMaj7 EMaj7
	Gb	Gb	Gbmin	Eadd9	Fbmin(add9) Emin(add9)	Fbsus2 Esus2	Ebmin	Ebb D	Dbmin(add11)	Dbsus4	Cbmin Bmin	Cb B	Bbbmin6 Amin6	Bbb6 A6	Abmin7	Ab7	Abbmin(Maj7) Gmin(Maj7)	AbbMaj7 GMaj7
Sharped Root	C#	C#	C#min	Badd9	Bmin(add9)	Bsus2	A#min Bbmin	A	G#min(add11)	G#sus4	F#min	F#	Emin6	E6	D#min7	D#7	Dmin(Maj7)	DMaj7
	D#	D#	D#min	C#add9	C#min(add9)	C#sus2	B#min Cmin	B	A#min(add11) Bbmin(add11)	A#sus4 Bbsus4	G#min	G#	F#min6	F#6	E#min7 Fmin7	E#7 F7	Emin(Maj7)	EMaj7
	F#	F#	F#min	Eadd9	Emin(add9)	Esus2	D#min	D	C#min(add11)	C#sus4	Bmin	B	Amin6	A6	G#min7	G#7	Gmin(Maj7)	GMaj7
	G#	G#	G#min	F#add9	F#min(add9)	F#sus2	E#min Fmin	E	D#min(add11) Ebmin(add11)	D#sus4 Ebsus4	C#min	C#	Bmin6	B6	A#min7 Bbmin7	A#7 Bb7	Amin(Maj7)	AMaj7

ACTIVITY

You can use Uncle Shane's Famous Chord Finder to replace chords in an existing chord progression or to search for a spicy chord when first creating a song. When songwriting, you can first map out a preliminary chord progression—but leave a blank space for "new" chords wherever you identify a focus note. Then, play the chord progression over and over, using replacement chords from the chart in that blank position.

You'll usually have one of three reactions:

1. That's works, but it is boring.
2. That terrible! and,
3. Ooo...that has possibility!

You'll be surprised at how many "Ooo" reactions you'll have. This method takes you out of your normal box and helps you find spicy replacements.

Let's practice this technique of finding interesting chords. For each given focus note/chord pair, use the Chord Finder to discover three alternate chords. Remember, you can use the focus note or the root of the given chord to find a replacement.

Key Note	Given Chord	Possible Alternate Chords		
D	G			
E	E			
A	F			
F♯	DMaj7			
F	G7			
C	Amin7			

YOUR NEXT SONG

Find a word or a phrase that you want to highlight in one of your previously written songs. Choose the melody note at the beginning of the measure, and go through Uncle Shane's Famous Chord Finder to discover the chord that creates the most prosody for that word or phrase.

CHAPTER 20

Ornament Chords

Employ complementary harmony shifts to color your arrangement.

An *ornament chord* is a brief excursion away from an anchor chord to a color/ ornament chord, and then back to that anchor chord. Incorporating ornament chords can be a great way to add momentary color to a chord progression.

For example, say you have a chord progression that is a C major chord for one measure.

Chord	C	C	C	C
Beat	1	2	3	4

You could play an ornament chord, such as the F chord shown in the following diagram, once or multiple times between any of the C chords, on any of those beats.

Chord	C	**F**	C	C
Beat	1	2	3	4

The ornament chord is relative to the anchor chord and can be outside of the song's key. You're just using it to provide a momentary burst of color.

EXAMPLE USING THE RELATIVE II MINOR

The relative II minor chord has a root a whole step above the anchor chord. For example, Dmin is the relative IImin for any C major or minor chord, as in:

Chord	C	Dmin	C	C
Beat	1	2	3	4

...or....

Chord	Cmin	Cmin	Dmin	Cmin
Beat	1	2	3	4

The relative II minor chord comes from gospel music, although you'll hear it used in an assortment of genres.

EXAMPLE USING RELATIVE ♭VII MAJOR

The relative ♭VII is major chord whose root is a whole step *below* the target chord. B♭ major is the relative ♭VII major for C, as in:

Chord	C	B♭	C	C
Beat	1	2	3	4

...or....

Chord	Cmin	Cmin	B♭	Cmin
Beat	1	2	3	4

Adding ♭VII gives a progression a darker tone, whether the I is major or minor.

Besides related IImin and ♭VII, you can use a variety of other chord types as ornament chords, as shown in this chart.

	Anchor Chord	**Ornament Chords**					**Anchor Chord**
		sus2	**sus4**	**Related IImin**	**Related IV**	**Related ♭7**	
Natural Root	A, Amin	Asus2	Asus4	Bmin	D	G	A, Amin
	B, Bmin	Bsus2	Bsus4	C♯min	E	A	B, Bmin
	C, Cmin	Csus2	Csus4	Dmin	F	B♭	C, Cmin
	D, Dmin	Dsus2	Dsus4	Emin	G	C	D, Dmin
	E, Emin	Esus2	Esus4	F♯min	A	D	E, Emin
	F, Fmin	Fsus2	Fsus4	Gmin	B♭	E♭	F, Fmin
	G, Gmin	Gsus2	Gsus4	Amin	C	F	G, Gmin
Flatted Root	A♭, A♭min	A♭sus2	A♭sus4	B♭min	D♭	G♭	A♭, A♭min
	B♭, B♭min	B♭sus2	B♭sus4	Cmin	E♭	A♭	B♭, B♭min
	C♭, C♭min	C♭sus2	C♭sus4	D♭min	E	B♭♭/A	C♭, C♭min
	D♭, D♭min	D♭sus2	D♭sus4	E♭min	G♭	C♭	D♭, D♭min
	E♭, E♭min	E♭sus2	E♭sus4	Fmin	A♭	D♭	E♭, E♭min
	G♭, G♭min	G♭sus2	G♭sus4	A♭min	C♭	F♭/E	G♭, G♭min
Sharped Root Root	C♯, C♯min	C♯sus2	C♯sus4	D♯min	F♯	B	C♯, C♯min
	D♯, D♯min	D♯sus2	D♯sus4	Fmin	G♯	C♯	D♯, D♯min
	F♯, F♯min	F♯sus2	F♯sus4	G♯min	B	E	F♯, F♯min
	G♯, G♯min	G♯sus2	G♯sus4	A♯min	C♯	F♯	G♯, G♯min

ACTIVITY

Here is a common chord progression: C G Amin F. The relative IImin for each of those chords are:

Anchor Chord	Ornament Chord (IImin)
C	Dmin
G	Amin
Amin	Bmin
F	Gmin

In this exercise, practice incorporating ornament chords into the given progression. Start by using the relative IImin on all of them. Then go through the list, mixing different ornament chord options.

	Beat			
Measure	**1**	**2**	**3**	**4**
1	Cmin	Cmin	?	Cmin
2	G	?	G	G
3	Amin	?	Amin	Amin
4	F	?	?	F

You don't have to use an ornament chord on every line with every chord, as in the preceding example. Find moments when you want to add color in your own chord progression.

The song "I'm Not in Love" (Eric Steward, Graham Gouldman; performed by 10 CCs) uses all three ornament chords we have been discussing throughout the arrangement. Listen for the background harmonies, which use the IImin and the IV chord. The ♭VII comes in at the end of the first verse.

YOUR NEXT SONG

Write a song featuring ornament chords—especially an ornament chord that contributes to prosody.

CHAPTER 21

Chord Permutations

Reorder a favorite chord progression to create engaging new variations.

There are four main ways you can alter a chord progression to create new permutations. In our examples, we'll use a four-chord progression. This technique will work for any number of chords in a progression.

C Amin G F

Here are the four chord permutation techniques. Starting with the original chord progression above, try the following techniques:

- **Flip the Middle:** Flip the order of the middle two chords; the first and last chord remain the same:
  C **G Amin** F
- **Return to Sender:** Replace the last chord with the starting chord:
  C Amin G **C**
- **Double Down:** Remove the existing last chord and play the next-to-last chord twice as long:
  C Amin **G G**
- **Off the Bench:** Trade the starting chord position with any other chord.

1. F Amin G C (Switched C and F)
2. Amin C G F (Switched C and Amin)
3. G Amin C F (Switched C and G)

You can then rearrange this new progression using any of the other techniques.

ACTIVITY

Write a four-chord progression, and apply all the techniques until you find a new appealing combination. Remember, you are evoking different musical emotional journeys—not just moving chords around.

YOUR NEXT SONG

Choose a chord progression from one of your Top 20 songs. Go through the permutations to create a new chord combination. Pay particular attention to the mood the new chord combination is creating for your own song.

CHAPTER 22

Harmonic Substitution

Modify your chords by replacing roots and/or 5's with color tones.

Here are some genius strategies to get you out of the rut of playing the same old triads and seventh chords.

Harmonic substitution is the practice of switching out some chord tones for others that have more color. Typically, the notes that get switched out are the root and 5. The ability to leave out some of those relatively predictable notes in favor of more colorful tones opens the door to tremendous creative freedom for prosody possibilities.

In a band situation, another player (such as the bass), or a MIDI voice, is likely to be sounding the root and 5, so the overall chord sound will still be heard if you leave them out. If you are just using a solo piano or guitar accompaniment:

- On piano, play the root with your left hand, and the chord voicings with your right hand.
- On guitar, play the root on either of the low strings, and the chord voicings in the remaining four high strings.

The way I use harmonic substitution is that after I've created a chord progression with standard major or minor chords, I will go back and look for moments where the arrangement might benefit from using relatively unconventional chord tones instead. I will then substitute those in to create more color.

In the following examples, I'm using versions of a C major or a C minor chord, but this technique applies to *any* major or minor chord. Also, you can use this approach for any chord voicing (i.e., note order, such as inversions, open/close voicings, etc.).

Understanding the theory behind harmonic substitution isn't as important as just moving your fingers to use a new chord. Don't worry about the complex chord symbol. Often, when I create chord charts for my songs, I will write a simple "C" chord, but still play one of the variations shown.

COMMON SUBSTITUTE NOTES

In major, you can substitute 9 for 1, 13 for 5, or add a major 7 (M7).

In minor, you can substitute 9 for 1, 11 for 5 (which has a gorgeous—and rarely heard—beauty), add a dominant 7 (♭7).

This chart shows some common substitutions for minor triads, major triads, and dominant 7 chords. Some chords are shown in multiple voicings.

Chord	Voicing 1	Voicing 2	Voicing 3	Substitution/Addition
C Major Triad	C E G			(given chord)
	1 3 5			
Cadd9	D E G	E G D		D for C
	9 3 5	3 5 9		9 for 1
C(add9,13)no5	E A D			D for C, A for G
	3 13 9			9 for 1, 13 for 5
CMaj7(add13)no5	B E A			A for G, adding B
	M7 3 13			6 for 5, adding M7
CMaj7(9,13)	E A B D	B D E A		D for C, A for G, adding B
	3 13 M7 9	M7 9 3 13		9 for 1, 13 for 5, adding M7

C Minor Triad	C E♭ G			(given chord)
	1 ♭3 5			
Cmin(add9)	D E♭ G	E♭ G D		D for C
	9 ♭3 5	♭3 5 9		9 for 1
Cmin(add11)no5	C E♭ F	E♭ F D	B♭ E♭ F	F for G, D for C, adding B♭
	1 ♭3 11	♭3 11 9	♭7 ♭3 11	11 for 5, 9 for 1, adding 7
Cmin7(add11)no5	E♭ F B♭	C E♭ F B♭		F for G, adding B♭
	♭3 11 ♭7	1 ♭3 11 9		11 for 5, adding ♭7
Cmin(11)no5	D E♭ F B♭			D for C, F for G, adding ♭7
	9 ♭3 11 9			9 for 1, 11 for 5, adding ♭7
Cmin9	D E♭ G B♭	E♭ G B♭ D	B♭ D E♭	D for C, adding ♭7
	9 ♭3 5 ♭7	♭3 11 ♭7 9	♭7 9 ♭3 5	9 for 1, adding ♭7

C7	C E G B♭			(given chord)
	1 3 5 ♭7			
C7(9,13)	E A B♭ D	B♭ D E A		D for C, A for G
	3 13 ♭7 9	♭7 9 3 13		9 for 1, 13 for 5
C7(♯9,♭13)	E A♭ B♭ D♯			D♯ for C, A♭ for G
	3 ♭13 ♭7 ♯9			♯9 for 1, ♭13 for 5

That last chord variation for C7, C7(♯9,♭13), is one that I wish someone would have shown me earlier. You can't use it all the time, but when you can, it is deliciously tense!

ACTIVITY

Choose a minor chord and a major chord that you use a lot in your songwriting, and using the preceding chart, go through the different options to hear how it sounds. Ask yourself what emotional change occurs with each voicing.

Then, extend this practice to a chord progression. Write just the chords for a new song that has the same chords in the verse and chorus. First, in the verse, use standard chords, and in the chorus, use the chart to find variations of those chords. Then do it the other way around, with the substitutions in the verse. What emotional effect do the different chord types suggest? Different voicings suggest different emotions. What do they mean to you?

YOUR NEXT SONG

Write a song based on the general progression from the Activity in this lesson. On a chord-by-chord basis, choose whether to use a standard chord or a harmonic substitution, based on the emotional impact you want for each lyric.

CHAPTER 23

Playing with Sus Chords

Use suspensions and inversions to transform lackluster chords progressions.

Replacing any chord with its equivalent sus2 or sus4 is a marvelous way to create new color in your songs. Sus chords are built using 1 2 5 or 1 4 5, rather than including the 3. This works great with all triads, major 7 chords, dominant 7 chords, and minor 7 chords.

Sus chords can have a dreamy, contemplative nature. They can also create an ambiguous tonal quality, as they are neither major or minor chords.

I use these as both an inspirational tool for composing and as an arranging tool to shore up a boring arrangement.

When I'm stuck, I'll grab a chord progression from a favorite song and replace one or more of chords with its sus2 or sus4 equivalent.

For example:

Original Chord	Sus Chord	Sus Chord Notes	Comment
C (triad)	Csus2	C D G 1 2 5	
	Csus4	C F G 1 4 5	
CMaj7	CMaj7sus2	C D G B 1 2 5 7	I love this chord, I use it as my ring tone!
	CMaj7sus4	C F G B 1 4 5 7	Notice this chord has a harsher sound.
C7 or Cmin7	C7sus2	C D G B♭ 1 2 5 ♭7	
	C7sus4	C F G B♭ 1 4 5 ♭7	
	C7sus2and4	C D F G B♭ 1 2 4 5 ♭7	

UNCLE SHANE'S SUS2/3 VOICING FOR MAJOR CHORDS

I want to share with you a voicing idea I've used on countless songs that sounds ridiculously good. Remember how in the sus chords we've removed the 3? Well, I love to put the 3 back, but as the bass note! It is a *marvelous* and original sound.

In chord notation, you'll often see a slash mark (/), which means your bass note is different than the root of the chord. For example: C/E means playing a C chord with an E in the bass. For the Uncle Shane's sus2/3 voicing to work:

- on the piano, play the sus2 chord (in any inversion) in the right hand, and the 3 in the left hand
- on guitar, play the 3 in one of the lower two strings.

Original Chord	Sus Chord	Sus Chord Notes		Comment
		Bass	Chord	
C (triad)	Csus2/E	E 3	C D G 1 2 5	Any chord voicing

You can do the same trick with any of the major 7 or dominant 7 chords that you've replaces with a sus2, as in:

Original Chord	Sus Chord	Sus Chord Notes		Comment
		Bass	Chord	
C7 or C7sus2	C7sus2/E	E 3	C D G B♭ 1 2 5 ♭7	Any chord voicing
CMaj7 or CMaj7sus2	Cmaj7sus2/E	E 3	C D G B 1 2 5 7	Any chord voicing

SUS CHORDS IN DISGUISE

These next delicious voicings aren't necessarily transferrable to every chord in every situation, but I wanted to share them anyway. They are easier on keyboard than guitar, but if you are arranging for a band, their notes can be divided among multiple players.

That dissonant whole-step sound of a sus2 chord is similar to a close-voicing 9 chord, which will also have the 3. So the chords in this section feel like sus chords, even though they aren't necessarily easily written as sus chords.

Here are two chord voicings I like that have a similar effect to the sus2.

Original Chord	Substitute Chord	Chord Notes		Comment
		Left	Right	
CMaj7	CMaj7no3/E	E 3	B C G 7 R 5	Notice the B (the major 7) is directly below the C
	CMaj9/B	B C 7 R	E G D 3 5 2	

I call this next voicing the "Buddy Hill Minor 7." Buddy Hill was my high school piano teacher. He was a brilliant professional musician in Las Vegas. Buddy showed me this chord voicing in 1983, and I've used it a million times. You really have to stretch your hands, but you'll love it as I do!

Original Chord	Substitute Chord	Chord Notes	
		Left	Right
Cmin	Cmin11	C G D 1 5 9	E♭ B♭ F ♭3 ♭7 11

Our last chord voicing, the "fancy V chord," is for dominant chords. It sounds particularly amazing as a replacement for the V or V7 chord in a song. The following example is for a G chord acting as the V chord in the key of C.

Original Chord	Substitute Chord	Chord Notes	
		Left	Right
G or G7	FMaj7/G	G 1	F A C E ♭7 9 11 13

ACTIVITY

In the above charts, we wrote all the examples in the key of C. These variations can of course be applied to any key. Grab a couple non-C chords that you are familiar with, and run through the different variation iterations. Take note of the different emotional shadings. Try these with both major and minor chords. Not all chords will work in all situations; this is just an exploration for thinking "outside the box." We are trying to bring more color into our songwriting arrangements.

YOUR NEXT SONG

Similar to the previous chapter, write a song based on a new progression. For each chord, choose whether to use a standard chord or a harmonic substitution, based on the emotional impact you want for each lyric. Remember that major 7 chords work well as substitutes for I and IV, and the pure sus2 and sus4 work well as substitutes for any major or minor chords. Try to use the V chord substitute voicings for your V chord. Add all these new variation ideas to your growing list of chord possibilities.

CHAPTER 24

Approach Chords

Create harmonic momentum using dominant and substitute dominant chords, and the related ♭VII chord.

You will often want to create motion and build momentum underneath certain lyrics, within harmonic phrases, and towards new song sections, such as a prechorus moving towards a chorus. You can do this by using approach chords.

Building momentum with approach chords requires a pairing of chords: a target chord (which provides stability) and its approach chord (which is unstable and creates the momentum).

First, identify the target chord underneath a lyric or musical moment where you want the musical momentum to lead. Then, you can add a chord or series of chords that have a sense of gravitational pull towards that target.

Once the target chord is established, there are three ways we can approach it: from dominant chords, substitute dominant chords, or the related ♭7 chord. Each of these has a triad color, a dominant 7 color, and a major 7 color.

Let's look at examples of each type, using a C triad as a target chord.

First, you can approach the C (root of the target chord, which can be major or minor) from a dominant position: a fifth above the root of the target chord. Then, choose one of the three flavors of approach chord (G triad, GMaj7, G7):

Approach: Dominant	Target
G triad	C
GMaj7	C
G7	C

Or, you can approach it from a substitute dominant position, which is a half step above the root of the approach chord (again, which can be major or minor, or any seventh chords previously discussed):

Approach: Substitute Dominant	Target
D♭ triad	C
D♭7	C
D♭Maj7	C

Or you can approach the root from a relative ♭VII chord, which is technically a ♭7 above the root, but it's easier to find and more musical if you approach from a whole step beneath the target chord:

Approach: Relative ♭7	Target
B♭ triad	C
B♭7	C
B♭Maj7	C

This chart shows the approaches towards the nine most common roots of target chords. (Some are listed enharmonically for ease.)

	(Target)	Approach Chords									Target
		Dominant			Substitute Dominant			♭7			
Natural	A	E	E7	EMaj7	B♭	B♭7	B♭Maj7	G	G7	GMaj7	A
	B	F♯	F♯7	F♯Maj7	C	C7	CMaj7	A	A7	AMaj7	B
	C	G	G7	GMaj7	D♭	D♭7	D♭Maj7	B♭	B♭7	B♭Maj7	C
	D	A	A7	AMaj7	E♭	E♭7	E♭Maj7	C	C7	CMaj7	D
	E	B	B7	BMaj7	F	F7	FMaj7	D	D7	DMaj7	E
	F	C	C7	CMaj7	F♯	F♯7	F♯Maj7	E♭	E♭7	E♭Maj7	F
	G	D	D7	DMaj7	A♭	A♭7	A♭Maj7	F	F7	FMaj7	G
Flat	A♭	E♭	E♭7	E♭Maj7	A	A7	AMaj7	G♭	G♭7	G♭Maj7	A♭
	B♭	F	F7	FMaj7	B	B7	Maj7	A♭	A♭7	A♭Maj7	B♭
	D♭	A♭	A♭7	A♭Maj7	D	D7	DMaj7	C♭	C♭7	C♭Maj7	D♭
	E♭	B♭	B♭7	B♭Maj7	E	E7	EMaj7	D♭	D♭7	D♭Maj7	E♭
	G♭	D♭	D♭7	D♭Maj7	G	G7	GMaj7	E	E7	EMaj7	G♭
Sharp	C♯	G♯	G♯7	G♯Maj7	D	D7	DMaj7	B	B7	BMaj7	C♯
	D♯	A♯	A♯7	A♯Maj7	E	E7	EMaj7	C♯	C♯7	C♯Maj7	D♯
	F♯	C♯	C♯7	C♯Maj7	G	G7	GMaj7	E	E7	EMaj7	F♯

ACTIVITY

Find a chord progression you like from your Top 20 Songs list. Treat the different chords of the progression as target chords. Using the preceding chart, experiment with approaching them with different flavors of approach chords. Pay note to how different combinations affect the progression's momentum and emotional result.

YOUR NEXT SONG

Write a song that uses a target chord and one of its flavors of approach chord in a key lyrical moment, where creating momentum positively affects the song's prosody.

CHAPTER 25

Approaching the Approach Chords

Use the II or ♭VI to extend momentum towards a target chord.

You can further extend the momentum and energy towards a target chord or new song section with an additional chord that approaches the approach chord. This approach-to-the-approach chord will be based on the root of the II or ♭VI relative to the target chord. Which iteration of II or ♭VI you use will depend on whether your target chord is based on a major or minor chord.

If you are approaching a major triad, major 7, or dominant 7 chord, use this chart to find the right approach to your approach.

Approaching the Approach	Approach (Dominant)	Target
IImin, IImin7	♭II, ♭II7	I, IMaj7, I7
II, II7		
♭VImin, ♭VImin7		
♭VI, ♭VI7		
IImin, IImin7	V, V7	
II, II7		
♭VImin, ♭VImin7		
♭VI, ♭VI7		

If you are approaching a minor triad or minor 7 chord, use this chart to find the right approach to your approach.

Approaching the Approach	Approach (Dominant)	Target
IImin, IImin7, IImin7♭5	♭II, ♭II7	Imin, Imin7
♭VImin, ♭VImin7, ♭VImin7♭5		
IImin, IImin7, IImin7♭5	V, V7	
♭VImin, ♭VImin7, ♭VImin7♭5		

For prosody, take note that the minor chords don't feel like they resolve until the progression reaches the target chord, while major approach-to-the-approach chords resolve immediately into their next chord. Think of the minor chord approach-to-the-approach as being more of a slow burn, while major chords are more like jump starts.

Chords	Target Chord Quality	Resolving Chord
Any minor triad or minor 7	Major or minor	Target
Any minor 7♭5	Minor	Target
Any major triad	Major or minor	Approach
Any dominant 7	Major or minor	Approach

Note: To extend the momentum even further back, you can add additional approach-to-the-approach chords.

Using the II as an approach chord lends a jazzy feel to the progression. Billy Joel is a master at using this technique in his songs, such as "New York State of Mind."

ACTIVITY

Find a chord progression from another song in your Top 20 Songs list. Find a major target chord and a minor target chord and experiment with both their approach and their approach-to-the-approach chords, using the charts in this lesson as your guide. Practice listening to how the approach-to-the-approach chord affects the final target chord.

YOUR NEXT SONG

Write a song that uses the approach-to-the-approach chord technique. Specifically, look for a moment in your song that would benefit from building momentum in this way.

Part III

Melody

I love discussing melody with songwriters, a topic few talk about. The next part of the book is a collection of some of my favorite techniques for building more expressive melodies that better contribute to the overall emotional intent of a song.

CHAPTER 26

The Melody Snippet

Initiate a brilliant original melody utilizing phrase snippets from your favorite songs.

A difficult aspect for many songwriters is coming up with an original and fresh melody for their song. This chapter aims at giving the struggling melody writer access to a host of melody ideas to use in their own songwriting.

Choose a Top 20 song, especially a song that has a melody that is appealing to you. We are going to find melody snippets that occur within the longer melodic phrases of that host song. You can then use those smaller snippets as the basis for your own melody.

Listen for a snippet about three to five notes long—not a signature melody in the song, but perhaps a vocal inflection, the end of a phrase, something interesting that happens in the middle or end of that phrase that is pleasing to your ear. Then pull out that melody snippet, and repeat it over the original chord progression. There can be multiple snippets in a single song. It is surprising how smaller snippets translate to chord progressions that differ from the original.

Once you find that interesting snippet, you will probably need to vary or embellish it when you add lyrics. Fortunately, there are a number of different techniques to help you through that process. These techniques can also be used in combination with each other.

- **Rhythmic position.** Move the snippet to start on a different beat or sub-beat of the measure.
- **Rhythmic variation.** Choose a note in the melody and change how long you hold it for.
- **Addition.** Add your own notes to the melody.
- **Subtraction.** Remove some notes from the melody.
- **Repetition.** Repeat notes or a sequence of notes within the melody.
- **Transposition.** Set your snippet starting on a higher or lower note. Keep all the subsequent notes of the snippet diatonic.
- **Inversion.** Change the melodic direction, so that instead of notes going up by an interval, they go down, and vice versa.
- **Retrograde.** Set the melody backwards.

- **Parallel major/minor switching.** Change a major key melody to minor, or vice versa.
- **Beginning/ending note.** Change the beginning or ending note, or both.

ACTIVITY

Choose a favorite song from your Top 20 Songs list that has a great melody. Listen for small three-to-five-note phrases that occur at the beginning, middle, or end of longer phrases. Remember, these can be vocal inflections or runs used by the lead vocalist. Use those three to five notes as your snippet. As you add lyrics, start by repeating the snippet on a new chord progression. Try varying your snippet using each of the suggested techniques. Combine your results in various ways to create longer melodies as needed.

YOUR NEXT SONG

Write a verse using a melodic snippet from a host song. Then write a chorus using a new melodic snippet from the same host song or a different song of your choosing. Toy with the two melodies using the techniques presented in the chapter, paying particular attention to creating prosody between the melodies and lyrics. Bonus: Do the same technique to write a bridge.

CHAPTER 27

Downbeat Word Placement

Move your melody horizontally to capitalize on key lyrics.

Placing a word on the downbeat of a line gives that particular word extra emphasis. We can take advantage of that emphasis to bring out different meanings of our titles/hooks.

The idea is to determine the most important word in a title/hook and place *that* word on the downbeat (i.e., beat 1 of a line).

Let's do an experiment to see how emphasizing different words can change the meaning of a phrase. Say the following phrase aloud, emphasizing a single word, and ask yourself what is implied by that version of the phrase. In practice, the emphasized word would be the word placed on the downbeat.

I *never said she stole my money.*

- You may have heard she stole my money, but you didn't hear it from me.

I **never** *said she stole my money.*

- I deny that I said she stole my money.

I never **said** *she stole my money.*

- I implied she stole my money, but I never expressed it aloud.

I never said **she** *stole my money.*

- SOMEONE stole my money, but I don't think it was her.

I never said she **stole** *my money.*

- She is in possession of my money, but she didn't acquire it through criminal means.

I never said she stole **my** *money.*

- She stole SOMEONE'S money; she just didn't steal mine!

I never said she stole my **money**.

- She took SOMETHING from me; it was just something other than my money.

Examples of songs that set important lyrics on the downbeat:

- "Brick House" (Lionel Richie, Milan Williams, Walter Orange, Ronald LaPread, Thomas McClary, William King; performed by the Commodores)
- "Warm on a Cold Night" (Andy Clutterbuck, James Hatcher, William Coutts; performed by Honne). Notice the emphasis on the word "warm."

ACTIVITY

Go through your Top 20 Songs list, and experiment with saying each title aloud. Emphasize different words of those titles. Notice how emphasizing different words changes the affect and meaning of the original lyric phase.

YOUR NEXT SONG

Identify one of your own titles/hooks. Repeat through it, emphasizing each one of its words. When you find an emphasis that creates the meaning that you want, place that word on the downbeat of the measure. This may require starting a phrase way before or after the downbeat.

CHAPTER 28

Starting and Ending Notes

Plan out how we start and end melody lines to create more prosody.

It's common to start a melody or new harmonic region on the tonic note or chord root. We're psychologically drawn to begin the starting note with the tonic note, and by default, it can become our melody starting and ending note. Starting on a stable note is not a bad thing, but there are other options. Let's think about the effect of the starting note and how different choices can influence the emotional impact of your song.

Consider three categories for starting and ending notes: resolved (stable), color, or unresolved.

- The stable, resolved notes are 1 and 5 of the scale. Stable notes show strong intent and are well grounded, and we are naturally drawn to them. They are very comfortable.
- The distinctive color notes are 2, 3, and 6. Color notes are lighter and more buoyant, and feel good to our ears. They inject personality into a melody.
- The unresolved notes are 4 and 7. Unresolved notes are tense and harsher to our ears, but this harshness can be haunting and beautiful in its own way. These notes are seeking resolution that you can either give or not give your listener.

When starting or ending the melody for a section, ask yourself, "Which category of note best adds prosody to the lyric?" Any of the categories might be an effective starting or ending point. Remember, you can mix or match starting and ending notes, such as starting colorful and ending stable, etc.

Here are my opinions about the general effects of each note.

Note	Shane's Personal Description	Song Example
1	Anchored and steady	"Son of a Preacher Man" (John Hurley, Ronnie Wilkins; performed by Dusty Springfield)
2	Deliciously wistful and haunting	"Yesterday" (Paul McCartney, John Lennon; performed by the Beatles)
3	Eager	"Postcards from Hell" (the Woods Brothers)
4	Pensive and vulnerable	"Still" (Lionel Richie)
5	Durable and poised	"Single Ladies" (Christopher Stewart, Terius Nash, Beyoncé Knowles, Thaddis Harrel; performed by Beyoncé)
6	Gentle wildness	"I Can't Make You Love Me" (James Allen Shamblin, Michael Barry Reid; performed by Bonnie Raitt)
7	Radiates reflective instability	"Stay" (Shane Adams)

These opinions are general guidelines. The emotional qualities of each note will of course change based on the chord supporting it. Remember, we are only talking about the starting and ending note.

ACTIVITY

Find a chord progression from your Top 20 songs, or one of your own, and sing only one of the notes throughout the entire chord progression. Listen how the different notes affect each chord throughout the progression. Go through all seven notes, paying attention to where it sounds special.

YOUR NEXT SONG

Write a song where you consciously start and end your melodic phrases based on how the starting and ending note affects the prosody of the lyric.

CHAPTER 29

Modes and Melody

Use the characteristic notes to shape the emotion of a section.

The modes can bring distinctive emotional colors to your melodies, which in turn make your lyrics more meaningful. As we discovered with chords, there are varying degrees of light and dark depending on which mode you use. Let's look at a chart that shows that range of light and dark. Each mode has a characteristic pitch (shown) that gives it a unique color.

	Mode	Character	Alterations	Characteristic Notes						
Major	**Lydian**	Bright	Sharp 4	C	D	E	F♯	G	A	B
				Expectant, anxious						
	Ionian	Neutral	(none)	C	D	E	F	G	A	B
				Happy, light, calm						
	Mixolydian	Less Bright	Flat 7	C	D	E	F	G	A	B♭
				Serious, somber, weighty						
Minor	**Dorian**	Dark	Flat 3, 7	C	D	E♭	F	G	A	B♭
				Impassioned, soulful, expressive						
	Aeolian	Darker	Flat 3, 6, 7	C	D	E♭	F	G	A♭	B♭
				Detached, secluded, sad, muted						
	Phrygian	Darkest	Flat 2, 3, 6, 7	C	D♭	E♭	F	G	A♭	B♭
				Pensive, contemplative, withdrawn, reflective						
	Locrian	(Unusable)	Flat 2, 3, 5, 6, 7	C	D♭	E♭	F	G♭	A♭	B♭
				Highly dissonant and unstable (rarely used)						

Similar to chords, to establish a modal quality in a song melody, you need to:

1. Establish the tonic.
2. Utilize the characteristic pitch, either in the melody, the harmony, or both.

Applying these rules specifically to melody, the tonic of a key is usually established in the chords, leaving you to utilize the characteristic pitch at some point in your melody, especially where it supports the meaning of your lyrics. You now have the options to establish the mode:

- melodically but not harmonically
- harmonically but not melodically
- both harmonically and melodically

ACTIVITY

Find a major key that you are comfortable playing and singing in, for example, the key of C. Choose or create a short melody of five or six notes. Write out the note numbers (or notation, if you prefer) of that melody.

Then go through an iterative process of changing one of the notes in your melody for a characteristic note of one of the modes, which you can find in this lesson's chart. How does this impact the emotional effect of the melody? What lyrics come to mind with each iteration, as you pay particular attention to the feel of the note you changed?

YOUR NEXT SONG

Write a simple chorus lyric with a repeated hook, followed by verses and a bridge. In the chorus, showcase that lyrical hook with a characteristic pitch from the mode of your choice that underscores and supports the intended emotion of your lyric.

Remember, the characteristic pitch doesn't necessarily *have to* showcase a key word or phrase, but it is fun when it does. As with all the other tools presented in this book, use the modes when they can help create more prosody for your song.

CHAPTER 30

Melodic One-Upmanship

Electrify your sections by employing melodic one-upmanship.

You can make your choruses feel more like points of arrival if you set the chorus melody—particularly its first note—higher than the verse melody that preceded it. This is called "melodic one-upmanship." The chorus starts at least one note higher than any note in the verse.

The concept of melodic one-upmanship is simple: you make sure the first melody note on the first important word in your chorus is at least one note higher than any note already sung in the previous section. You'll be amazed at how much this elevates the impact of your chorus.

A more extreme example of melodic one-upmanship is to write the *entire* chorus melody higher than the verse melody. If you've already written your verse and chorus and find they are in the same melodic territory, try either lowering your entire verse melody, or raising your entire chorus melody.

If you are feeling especially rebellious, do the opposite: have your verse melody higher than your chorus melody. The idea is that your listeners will hear something melodically new when the chorus arrives.

You can apply this same concept to a bridge, starting it with a new higher note that hasn't been sung yet in the verse or chorus.

ACTIVITY

Write two lyrical lines. Line 1 is a single verse-style line, serving as the last line of a verse. Line 2 contains the title/hook, serving as the first line of your chorus.

Write melodies for these two lines in the following ways:

1. Line 2 starts one note higher than any note you sang in the first line.
2. The entire melody of line 2 is higher than line 1.
3. The entire melody of line 2 is lower than line 1.

YOUR NEXT SONG

Write a song where your chorus is emphasized using one of the previous techniques. At a minimum, the first note of the chorus should be new.

CHAPTER 31

Melodic Holes

Employ verse melodic holes for maximum chorus melody impact.

In the spirit of hearing new melody notes in your chorus to make it stand apart from the verse, you can incorporate what I call *melodic holes* in your verse.

To simplify this, let's pretend that your melody only has seven notes—the same number as in a scale.

1 2 3 4 5 6 7

If you sing *all* seven of those notes in the verse, there is nothing new for the chorus. A *melodic hole* is an intentional non-sung note that you save as the first note for your chorus. So imagine that seven-note range again, but this time leave out leave out note number 5 and use it for your first note of the chorus....

1 2 3 4 (5) 6 7

It doesn't mean you can't sing the remaining six notes in your chorus. Just *start* your chorus with a new note, making it sound fresh to your listeners.

If you leave two holes in your verse, this insures that you can have a new starting note for your chorus *and* your bridge. Just make sure you don't sing that second hole in your chorus, saving it for the bridge.

Tip: Pentatonic scales are like major scales that already come with two holes.

Major Pentatonic:	1	2	3	(4)	5	6	(7)
Minor Pentatonic:	1	(2)	♭3	4	5	(6)	♭7

ACTIVITY

Practice singing all seven notes of a scale in your vocal range. Experiment with skipping over one or two of those notes, in anticipation of using one of the missing notes to start the chorus and the other missing note to start the bridge.

YOUR NEXT SONG

Write a song that purposefully leaves out a note in the verse, which you will then use as the first note of your chorus. Alternatively, write a song that purposefully leaves out two notes in the verse, so that you use the missing notes to begin your chorus and bridge.

Feel free to stick with the seven-note scale you used in the activity or expand the melody range higher and/or lower, in accordance with your comfort of using more notes.

CONCLUSION

Thanks for allowing me to accompany you on your songwriting journey. I hope the content of this book allows you to better express your best emotional self through your songwriting, regardless of style or genre. The world is absolutely a better place with your music in it.

I wish you love and luck.

Go write!

ABOUT THE AUTHOR

Photo by Gregg Roth

Shane Adams, president of Artist Accelerator, is a Nashville resident and Las Vegas native. He is an award-winning songwriter, producer, and author of *The Singer-Songwriter's Guide to Recordings in the Home Studio*. Shane's artists have hundreds of thousands of listens on streaming services.

Shane attended Berklee College of Music and became a founding instructor at Berklee Online. He is now an Associate Professor mentoring master degree candidates at Berklee NYC. Shane is also a founding songwriting and music production instructor and course developer for Interlochen Online. He has served in various capacities at several record label and music publishers.

Shane has two GRAMMY nominations as a music educator. He received the Tennessee Songwriters Association's highest honor: the Hallman Award. In 2013, Shane was named the Music Industry Professional of the Year by Chowan University. Shane has also received the Country Music Hall of Fame's Top Ten Hitmaker award for co-developing the Taylor Swift Education Center's Words & Music program and Songwriting 101 program, which have taught over 200,000 kids to write and record music.

Shane is an internationally recognized songwriting expert and a mentor for hundreds of aspiring and professional writers. He is a frequent guest on many music-oriented podcasts. His *Quick Songwriting Tips* on YouTube have over 500,000 views.